≡ STRONG WOMEN ≡

Published in 2023 by Welbeck
An imprint of Welbeck Non-Fiction Limited
part of Welbeck Publishing Group
Offices in: London – 20 Mortimer Street, London W1T 3JW &
Sydney – Level 17, 207 Kent St, Sydney NSW 2000 Australia
www.welbeckpublishing.com

Text © Suzanne Wrack, 2023
Design © Welbeck Non-Fiction Limited, 2023
Illustrations © Izabela Kacprzak

A catalogue record for this book is available from the British Library.

ISBN: 978 1 80279 225 6

10 9 8 7 6 5 4 3 2 1

Printed in China

MIX
Paper | Supporting
responsible forestry
FSC® C020056
FSC
www.fsc.org

STRONG WOMEN

50 STORIES OF INSPIRATIONAL ATHLETES AT THE TOP OF THEIR GAMES

SUZANNE WRACK

WELBECK

INTRODUCTION

Women have rarely, if ever, been naturally and instinctively included in sport. At times they have been banned or restricted from many, if not all, sports. Historically, sport was the preserve of men, both a pastime for the wealthy and a morale and fitness-booster for the working masses.

E ven as the benefits of sport to both mental and physical health became increasingly investigated and widely known, it was still not considered suitable for women to participate in a wide variety of sports, certainly not at a professional or elite level. More recently, for women, exercise was done to lose weight, to pursue the perfect bikini body, and not for frivolous fun, mental stimulation, or any of the many benefits that team sport can provide.

So, throughout history, every woman pulling on spikes, lacing up boots, picking up a racquet, engaging in sport in any way, was considered a rebel. Sometimes conscious rebels, using the huge

influence and power of sport to aid women's rights more broadly, sometimes picking up the baton as the barriers went up against their often simple desire to participate, and sometimes completely unconscious rebels, influencing attitudes just by being excellent at their craft in a world that wasn't accepting.

The stories of hugely influential sportswomen are often lost, their names unknown, their Wikipedia pages blank. The world is waking up to the value and joy that can be found in watching and engaging with women's sport, but this is a new phenomenon. For too long women's sport and its stars have been on the fringes of society, garnering small niche followings and struggling for wider or long-lasting recognition.

Ask anyone to reel off a list of some of the all-time greats or most influential male athletes and the names roll off the tongue: Pelé, Diego Maradona, Ayrton Senna, Sachin Tendulkar, Jackie Robinson, Michael Jordan, Ronaldo, Tiger Woods, Muhammad Ali, Pete Sampras, Kareem Abdul-Jabbar, Michael Phelps, Joe Montana, Ty Cobb, Sugar Ray Robinson, Babe Ruth, Wayne Gretzky, and on and on we could go. Everyone knows their names, but also their stories.

In this book we look at 50 sportswomen who stood out from the crowd, either for how they used their platform, their sporting prowess,

or both. Here are women whose names and stories are more widely known, such as tennis and equality giant Billie Jean King and World Cup equal pay campaigner and LGBTQ+ rights advocate Megan Rapinoe, and also the names and stories of the lesser-known pioneers of women's sport, such as the first Black woman to play softball professionally, Betty Chapman, and Paralympic swimmer Béatrice Hess, who broke nine world records and won seven gold medals at the Sydney 2000 Olympic Games. We look at those who fought for the right to run, Boston Marathon runner Kathrine Switzer, the right to play at Lord's, cricketer Rachael Heyhoe Flint, and the right to compete at the Olympics, Frenchwoman Alice Milliat. We also feature those who highlighted the mental health struggles of athletes, such as Simone Biles and Naomi Osaka, those who challenged different forms of abuse within sport such as former Afghanistan women's national team captain Khalida Popal and footballer Kaiya McCullough.

We are singing the praises and impact of individuals, and that is important, but it is also important to contextualize their achievements and histories. They are all products of their times, backgrounds, experiences, and the people around them. If they had not existed, would progress have not been made? No, but developments may have taken a different route or a longer or shorter path.

That's why looking at the conditions which shaped the individual are important, which we try to do here, discussing their influences and upbringings as much as their own achievements. It's when the right individuals intersect with a moment in time and a specific set of circumstances that change happens.

Writing this book has not been easy. There is a huge dearth of information about so many of these brilliant athletes that in some cases we have only skimmed the surface of their lives, lives which could likely fill books in their own right. It is a tragedy that there is so little information on key women in the history of sport, let alone those less influential. It has meant that, in cutting down the list to 50, some women, whose achievements would often be summarized in a sentence and nothing more, did not make it in. It is also likely that the stories of many pioneering women athletes who merit inclusion in this book have been lost entirely, with so many of these women reliant on family members or self-funded amateur researchers or hobbyists to unearth evidence of their lives and achievements.

BETTY CHAPMAN

The earliest record of women playing organized baseball in the United States dates back to 1866, when Vassar College in Poughkeepsie, upstate New York, became the first university to field women's baseball teams.

It took another 77 years before the first women's professional baseball league, the All-American Girls Professional Baseball League, which played a hybrid of softball and baseball in its first season, was launched by the owner of the Chicago Cubs, Philip K. Wrigley (the chewing gum magnate). The motivation for founding the league was familiar, with Wrigley using the league to keep the ballparks full during World War I with the men's baseball ranks depleted by the conflict.

More than 200 women were asked to try out after the amateur leagues across the country were scoured for talent and around 60 were chosen to make up the first roster. This was not a league for the rough and ready, the rules were strict. The players had to attend Helena

> ## "FEMININITY IS THE KEYNOTE OF OUR LEAGUE; NO PANTS-WEARING, TOUGH-TALKING FEMALE SOFT-BALLER WILL PLAY ON ANY OF OUR FOUR TEAMS."
>
> **Max Carey**

Rubinstein's evening charm school lessons, where they would learn etiquette, personal hygiene and appropriate dress codes. In the ballpark, their uniform was comprised of short-sleeved tunics with a belt. The rules stated that the skirt could not be shorter than six inches above the knee and players could be fined for not following other league rules, which included no short hair, no smoking or drinking in public places, no trousers, and the wearing of lipstick at all times.

Teams such as the Minneapolis Millerettes, Rockford Peaches, Grand Rapids Chicks, Fort Wayne Daisies, Kalamazoo Lassies, Peoria Redwings, Milwaukee Chicks, Muskegon Lassies and Chicago Colleens competed in the league.

"Femininity is the keynote of our league; no pants-wearing, tough-talking female softballer will play on any of our four teams," said Major League Baseball Hall of Fame inductee Max Carey, who was manager of the Milwaukee Chicks in 1944 and president of the AAGPBL.

As in the men's Major Leagues, there was informal segregation, where there were no formal rules against Black players but they were kept out of the pro game, and so none were recruited to the AAGPBL. The "colour line" in professional baseball was broken by Jackie Robinson in 1946 when he signed with the Brooklyn Dodgers.

Much less known is Betty Chapman who, five years later, would tread the same barrier-breaking path as Robinson, becoming the first Black woman to play professional softball in 1951. Chapman was far from the first Black woman to play baseball or softball. Women had been playing as amateurs for decades and in 1883 two teams, formed by a white barber, John Lang (who had also set up a number of teams of Black men and a Chinese team), using the name Dolly Varden were filled entirely by Black women. The *Delaware County Daily Times* called the first game between the teams "a failure," despite a large and enthusiastic crowd. The teams were disbanded after less than a year with the novelty of Black women playing baseball not profitable enough for Lang as it could not circumvent the ingrained racism and sexism of the time.

Chapman did not play in the AAGPBL, but played for Admiral Music Maids in the Chicago-based National Girls Baseball League, which was founded one year later to rival the AAGPBL. It offered bigger salaries and did not place the same strict rules on players. The NGBL existed for 10 years, frequently attracting more than half a million fans annually and, according to former player Freda Savona, the team drew bigger attendances than the Chicago White Sox MLB team.

While Robinson is one of the most well-known Black American athletes, whose story has been widely told, little is known of Chapman beyond that she was an outfielder and played for the Music Maids – or of the NGBL's Chinese-American player Gwen Wong and Japanese-American Nancy Ito.

THE NOVELTY OF BLACK WOMEN PLAYING BASEBALL WAS NOT PROFITABLE ENOUGH... TO CIRCUMVENT THE INGRAINED RACISM AND SEXISM OF THE TIME.

ANN GLANVILLE

In 1870, an image of a women's double sculls race graced the cover of the American political magazine *Harper's Weekly*. That image presents one of the earliest examples of women's competitive rowing.

The liberal arts college Wellesley, in Massachusetts, was the first educational institution to launch a women's team in the late 1800s; meanwhile, in 1892, a group of four women in San Diego founded what is believed to be the oldest existing all-women rowing club, the ZLAC Rowing Club.

One of the earliest relative superstars of women's rowing in Britain was Ann Glanville. Her route into rowing came out of necessity: when her husband John Glanville, from a long line of watermen in Cornwall, fell seriously ill, and she had to step in to support their family. The couple had 14 children to feed, so Ann learned his trade and a life on the water began to take shape.

"It is likely that Ann worked as a waterwoman between 1815 and 1850, rowing goods and passengers about the Tamar estuary and its creeks," wrote Terry Cummings in his book *Ann Glanville: The Myths and Facts*. "Through this work she developed the muscle and skill to earn a living. The arrival of paddle steamers on the river from around 1830 threatened the watermen and women's trade and

this led to the water-folk earning money racing at local regattas. A winning team could share a prize of £3–4."

Glanville formed a crew of four women to row in local regattas and also compete around Britain. Wearing caps and dresses, Glanville and her crew were not there just to make up the numbers; at an event in Fleetwood, Glanville was congratulated by the watching Queen Victoria after her team beat an all-male crew.

"The first mention of Ann Glanville is in 1833 at the Port of Plymouth Royal Regatta when her team was second in a four-oared gig race. From this point it seems that Ann and her crew were rarely beaten," wrote Cummings.

"In 1833, the names of the team captains and winners were Ann Glanville, Mary Glanville, Mary Jones and Susan Screech.

"By 1841, women's racing had become one of the main attractions at local regattas and for some 20 years, Saltash women were the elite."

One report, in *The Plymouth, Devonport and Stonehouse Herald*, said of the 1839 Sutton Pool Regatta: "The Saltash ladies as usual created the greatest attraction; they 'gave way' in fine style, and Ann Glanville, the heroine of a 'thousand races', came in victorious in the principal gig race. The style in which these 'water nymphs' managed their boats was greatly admired…. [They] were enthusiastically cheered by the spectators afloat and ashore."

In 1842, on the paddle steamer *Brunswick* and then the paddle steamer *Grand Turk*, Glanville and her crew, Glanville, Harriett Hosking,

"ANN GLANVILLE, THE HEROINE OF A 'THOUSAND RACES', CAME IN VICTO-RIOUS IN THE PRINCIPAL GIG RACE."

Devonport and Stonehouse Herald

Jane House and Amelia Lee, headed to France to compete in a re-gatta in Le Havre. However, the male crews in France did not want to compete against the women "for reasons of chivalry", and instead a team of sailors from the *Grand Turk* raced against the women. Word of the ambitions of the women from Saltash spread and there was a crowd of around 20,000 to watch the regatta, which the women won comfortably.

Tales of her exploits on the water were embellished by Glanville, who revelled in her celebrity status.

She died on June 6, 1880 and was buried in St Stephen's, where a Royal Marines band played the funeral march. A newspaper noted: "A noted 'character' has just died in the person of Ann Glanville. Her name is as familiar to a great many visitors to the town as a household word. The old lady enjoyed good health down to Saturday last, but on that day she was taken with a seizure, and succumbed early on Sunday morning at the age of 84. Her prowess as a rower is widely known, she being one of the 'ladies' crew' who 'beat the Frenchmen' some years ago at Calais, and also one of the yearly 'attractions' at the Saltash Regatta in the women's race. It was one of her weaknesses to tell how she had been patronized by Royalty having joked with the Duke of Edinburgh 'many a time'."

SAM KERR

Sam Kerr hates the spotlight, yet there is no avoiding it. "It's my job to score goals," she said, deflecting the attention from herself in an interview with the *Guardian*. "It's one of those things that's a good individual achievement, but if I can help my team win titles, that's the main thing."

Kerr's CV is staggering. The Australian football player has won the Golden Boot on three continents and is her country's record goal scorer (male or female).

Playing in both the Australian W-League and National Women's Soccer League in the US, Kerr was top scorer for Perth Glory in Australia in 2017–18 and 2018–19 and in America in 2017 – for Sky Blue – 2018 and 2019 – both with Chicago Red Stars. In 2021–21, her first full season in England, with Chelsea, she beat Arsenal forward Vivianne Miedema to the FA Women's Super League Golden Boot.

She has won the W-League title twice and two FA Women's Super League titles, two League Cups and one FA Cup with Chelsea.

At the AFC Women's Asian Cup in India in 2022, Kerr passed Tim Cahill's 50 goals for Australia when she scored five times in her country's opening match, an 18–0 defeat of Indonesia. That moment was all the more poignant for Kerr, as her father was born in India.

"I've been speaking to my family about ways I could help be a role model for young Indian girls," she said in a column for the BBC prior to the tournament. "My family's been in Australia 40 years now and I still don't know a

whole lot about India. I'm really proud to be Indian and love my skin colour and love my 'Indian complexion', as my nana says."

Things could have been very different. Kerr was a standout Australian Rules football player when she was young. Sam's father Roger – the son of a featherweight boxer father and basketball-playing mother – and older brother Daniel were both professional Aussie Rules players. Her uncle was a champion jockey – J.J. Miller rode Galilee to victory in the 1966 Melbourne Cup.

"I was a late bloomer so I didn't get into football until I was 12. I grew up playing Aussie Rules but my mum and dad stopped me from playing after I started coming home with black eyes and a bloodied face. My cousin was playing football so I thought I'd try it – and I hated every second of it," she told the BBC. "It wasn't until I was 15 and I got identified by the national team that I realized I was pretty good and could go somewhere. Up until that point I had just been playing with boys."

Now, Kerr is one of the most decorated players in women's football, but it is her attitude as a player on and off the pitch that has won her a huge following. After Australia came from 2–0 down to beat Brazil 3–2 in the team's second group match at the 2019 World Cup in France, following a shock 2–1 defeat to Italy in the team's opening fixture, Kerr was defiant. "There was a lot of critics talking about us, but we're back, so suck on that one," she said in the post-match interview. It went viral.

"One game was not gonna derail our World Cup hopes – and that's why it was so frustrating for us because instead of the media being (like), 'we can turn this around', it turned negative on us and it only fuelled us, so thank you," she continued.

"THERE ARE NO HIERARCHIES, THERE ARE NO CLIQUES, IT IS EVERYONE TOGETHER. WE ARE FIT AND WE ARE FAST. THAT'S WHERE WOMEN'S FOOTBALL IS GOING AT THE MOMENT. IT IS FAST AND AGGRESSIVE."

Sam Kerr

That passion and a mischievousness is what has made her loved. She is playful. After Chelsea celebrated winning the WSL, she did her pitch-side interview clutching a beer. Later, she would post on Instagram below a picture of teammates Pernille Harder and Magda Eriksson, who are a couple, "I LOVE YOU GUYS", "ADOPT ME" and "ERRRMAGOD". In 2022, another clip of the forward went viral again, when she nonchalantly strolled close to a pitch invader before barging him to the ground during Chelsea's 0–0 draw with Juventus in the group stage of the UEFA Women's Champions League.

Openly in a same-sex relationship with US women's national team player Kristie Mewis, and previously in a relationship with former teammate Nikki Stanton, Kerr has proved an inspiration to many.

HÉLÈNE DE POURTALÈS

Hélène de Pourtalès was born Helen Barbey in New York into an extremely wealthy family in April 1868. Her parents were Henry Issac Barbey, a Swiss banker, and Mary Barbey, whose father was Pierre Lorillard III, grandson of Pierre Abraham Lorillard, the founder of the Lorillard Tobacco Company in 1760 and one of the first people described in US newspapers as a millionaire.

B arbey spent her summers in Switzerland and she developed a passion for sailing as she spent the majority of her time yachting. Her family had a history in the sport. Her uncle, Pierre Lorillard IV, who owned thoroughbred racehorses and worked in the family's tobacco business, is believed to have helped make Rhode Island's Newport a yachting centre, with his steam yacht *Radha* and schooner *Vesta*.

She married Swiss sailor Count Hermann Alexander de Pourtalès in the American church of Saint-Trinité in Paris in 1891. A former captain in the Cuirassiers de la Garde regiment in the Prussian Army, he was a 44-year-old widower with five children, while she was 23. The pair had three daughters and sailed together in regattas.

HER FAMILY HAD A HISTORY IN THE SPORT.

Sailing was due to be in the Athens 1896 Olympic Games, but the regatta was cancelled so it made its debut in 1900. At Paris 1900, there were eight sailing classes and races took place on the Seine near Meulan and in the north Atlantic off the coast of Le Havre in the north-west of the country. Around 150 sailors and 64 boats took part from six nations. Among them were Hélène, Hermann and his nephew, Bernard. She was the only woman to take part in the sailing and one of the first women to compete at the Olympics, the first edition to allow women competitors.

Female athletes could compete in five events: golf, tennis, sailing, croquet and equestrian. As well as competing herself, de Pourtalès watched the golf, where her husband's cousin Jacques was a course referee. Aboard Swiss boat *Lérina*, de Pourtalès became the first woman to win an Olympic gold medal. Nine boats started the two

SHE WAS THE ONLY WOMAN TO TAKE PART IN THE SAILING AND ONE OF THE FIRST WOMEN TO COMPETE AT THE OLYMPICS.

THE SWISS TEAM, HELMED BY HERMANN WITH HÉLÉNE AND BERNARD AS CREW, FINISHED TWO SECONDS AHEAD OF FRENCH BOAT MARTHE.

races in the 1–2 ton class with 22 sailors involved in travelling the 19km course. Medals were given for each race.

There was reportedly very little wind for the first race on 22 May, making the conditions problematic, but the Swiss team, helmed by Hermann with Hélène and Bernard as crew, finished two seconds ahead of French boat *Marthe*. In the second race, on 25 May, the lightest boat competing, the 1.041-ton German boat *Aschenbrödel* ("Cinderella") finished 26 seconds ahead of *Lérina*, which finished in the silver medal position.

LILY PARR

During the First World War, the Admiralty and War Office approached various factories about converting to munitions production as Britain struggled to cope with the needs of war. One of those factories was the Dick, Kerr Company. Founded by Scotsmen William Bruce Dick and John Kerr, by 1890, the company had factories in Glasgow, Liverpool, Newcastle, Barrow-in-Furness, Cardiff and Hamburg.

In 1893, the company bought a factory in Preston which supplied tramway equipment and rolling stock and, by 1919, had built approximately 50 locomotives.

Making the switch to munitions meant equipment had to be replaced and the first shells were eventually bonded in 1915.

If the war needed munitions, the factories needed staff. As men, young and old, were enlisted to fight, women were recruited into the factories to keep the war effort alive. The "Munitionettes" worked in intense and dangerous conditions and, in order to maintain morale, female welfare supervisors were also recruited. One of the activities prompted was football, so factories across the country developed teams and the Dick, Kerr factory was no different. In tea and lunch breaks the women and girls participated in outdoor football kick-arounds. In October 1917, after a heavy run of poor results, the Dick, Kerr men's team, manned by young apprentices, was teased by some of the women players and

challenged to a match. The result of the match, which took place in Penwortham, is not known, but it gave birth to a women's team that became one of England's most decorated women's teams of the period.

On Christmas Day 1917, the team played a match at Preston North End's Deepdale stadium against the Arundel Coulthard Factory to raise money for the Moor Park Military Hospital. The match attracted 10,000 spectators and raised £600.

This was the start of a fantastic charity fund-raiser. Dick, Kerr Ladies XI raised hundreds of pounds in games up and down the country for injured servicemen or other local war charities, and also competed internationally. In 1920, Dick, Kerr Ladies played four games in England against a French team and then travelled to France to play in Paris, Roubaix, Le Havre and Rouen. The team drew big crowds and made a big name for themselves and, on Boxing Day in 1920, a match against rivals St Helen's Ladies attracted a crowd of 53,000 to Everton's Goodison Park.

In 1920, shortly after the tour of France, a young St Helen's player had caught the eye of team manager Alfred Frankland. That player would go on, in recent years at least, to be the face of the team. Born in 1905, Lily Parr debuted for her local team in St Helen's at 14.

By the time she was recruited by the famous Dick, Kerr Ladies, the team had played 123 games and attracted more than 1.25 million spectators. Parr worked in the factory and lived with another player, Alice Norris.

In September 1921, following a game against Coventry, the *Derby Daily Telegraph*, under the headline "From Fun to Cheers", said that fans "began to look at things from a different viewpoint when

"LILY PARR ... CAN BOOT A BALL FURTHER THAN ANY LADY IN THE COUNTRY."

Dundee Evening Telegraph

Lily Parr tricked her way, by deft footwork, past a couple of defenders and shot the ball goalwards with surprising force."

Days later, the *Dundee Evening Telegraph* wrote that: "Lily Parr, the sixteen-year-old outside left, can boot a ball further than any lady in the country."

On New Year's Day 1921, the teenager was shifted from left-back to left-wing and she thrived, scoring a hat-trick. She scored 108 goals in her first year with the team, second behind Florrie Redford, who netted 170 times.

The Football Association, however, was far from impressed by the success of Dick, Kerr Ladies in particular and women's football in general. In December 1921, the FA banned women's football from all affiliated grounds, effectively pulling the rug out from under for women's football and its dominant team, Dick, Kerr Ladies. Despite the ban, Dick, Kerr Ladies and many other teams continued to play, but they were forced to go underground, playing matches in parks and rugby grounds and, as a result, crowds shrunk. Parr still went on to score around 1,000 goals across a career spanning 33 years.

Since her death, in 1978, Parr has become a figurehead for the uncovered history of the Dick, Kerr Ladies team, but she was far from a solo star. Many other players, such as Redford and Joan Whalley, were as big, if not bigger. However, the story of Parr – who once broke a man's arm when taking a penalty against him and now has a permanent display in the National Football Museum in Manchester – was the one told first and as a result, her face has come to represent the history of the Dick, Kerr Ladies team.

ALICE MILLIAT

Few have pioneered the involvement of women in sports, a breadth of sports, more doggedly than Frenchwoman Alice Milliat. Born Alice Million in Nantes in 1884, her parents were not aristocratic, but were not poor either. Both were grocers, though her mother later worked as a seamstress and her father in an office.

Aged 20, Million moved to England, where she took to the water, picking up rowing, and also met her husband, Joseph Milliat. Sadly, Joseph died in 1908, after which Alice travelled and became proficient in several languages. She started working as a translator and in sport, as well as rowing, also played hockey and tried her hand at swimming.

Milliat was a passionate advocate for women's sport. She did not exist in isolation; during the First World War, as the men went to fight, women went out to work in factories and on the land, and a number of this newly liberated gender took up sport for recreation. Milliat's journey in sports leadership began shortly before the outbreak of the war, in 1912, when she got involved in a club called Fémina Sport and she became president in 1915. Initially the club was a gymnastics club but it expanded to include various team sports and athletics.

In 1917 Milliat had her fingers in a number of sporting pies. "Women's sport has its place in social life in the same way as men's sport," she said. At the same time, she helped found the Fédération des Sociétés Féminines Sportives de France and also organized a

women's football tournament. In 1920 she pulled together a Parisian football team that travelled to England and played the unstoppable Dick, Kerr Ladies in one of the earliest international women's football tournaments. Milliat's team played four games across the Channel, at Preston North End's Deepdale, at Stockport, in Manchester and at Stamford Bridge in London and then hosted the English team in Paris, Roubaix, Le Havre and Rouen.

Women were allowed to compete in the second edition of the modern Olympic Games in 1900 but only in golf and tennis in terms of individual events. In 1904 women's archery was included and by the 1908 Games in London, 37 women competed in archery, tennis and figure skating. Swimming and diving were added for the 1912 Games but archery and figure skating were removed. Archery was back for the 1920 Games.

Frustrated by the lack of opportunities for women to compete in the Olympic Games, ahead of the 1924 Games in Paris, Milliat appealed to the International Association of Athletics Federations (IAAF) for the inclusion of women's track and field events. The request was knocked back. Instead, Milliat helped to organize a five-day multi-sport Women's Olympiad, which was first held in 1921. Around 100 women from five countries – France, Italy, Switzerland, the United Kingdom and Norway – competed in Monaco and the events were: 60m, 250m, 800m, 4 x 75m relay, 4 x 175m relay, hurdles, high jump, long jump, javelin, shot put, basketball, gymnastics, pushball and rhythmic gymnastics.

Later that year, Milliat founded the Fédération Sportive Féminine Internationale and launched the 1922 Women's Olympic Games, which were later held that year and in 1926, 1930 and 1934. According to Florence Carpentier, author of *Alice Milliat: A Feminist Pioneer for Women's Sport*, the Women's World Games were an alternative to the Women's Olympiad. It is believed that the vice-president of the French Athletics Federation, Marcel Delabre, who was on the organizing committee of the Women's Olympiad, saw the Women's Olympiad as a way of controlling the development of women's athletics.

Milliat's Women's Olympic Games took place in Paris, the home of the "father of the modern Olympics" and founder of the International Olympic Committee Pierre de Coubertin, and included representatives from the United States, Great Britain, Switzerland, Czechoslovakia and France. Around 20,000 spectators watched 11 athletics events.

For the second, third and fourth editions, the name was changed to the Women's World Games. Milliat agreed to amend the name, which had infuriated the IOC and IAAF in exchange for 10 women's track and field events being included in the 1928 Olympics programme. However, the IOC backtracked and included only five.

After the 1934 Women's World Games, Milliat demanded an equal number of women's events in the Olympic Games or the control of all women's events should be handed over to the Fédération Sportive Féminine Internationale. In 1936 the IAAF voted to take over women's athletics and promised to add three more women's events to the Olympics athletics programme to take the total to nine, but this was too late for the Berlin Games. At the London Games in 1948, Fanny Blankers-Koen benefited from the change Milliat and her peers fought for and wrote her name into the history books by winning four gold medals.

Interviewed in *Independent Woman* magazine in 1934, Milliat said: "Women's sports of all kinds are handicapped in my country by the lack of playing space. As we have no vote, we cannot make our needs publicly felt, or bring pressure to bear in the right quarters. I always tell my girls that the vote is one of the things they will have to work for if France is to keep its place with the other nations in the realm of feminine sport."

BABE DIDRIKSON ZAHARIAS

"My goal was to be the greatest athlete who ever lived," Babe Didrikson Zaharias said of her ambitions as a teenager.

B orn Mildred Ella Didrikson, in Texas, to Norwegian immigrant parents, she claimed she was given the nickname "Babe", after Babe Ruth, after hitting five home runs in a children's baseball game. Growing up, she was a sports fiend, playing anything and everything she could. She excelled in athletics and basketball, but also played pool and bowled. She defied perceptions of femininity and womanhood, and was known for her athleticism. Didrikson's first job after high school was working as a secretary in an insurance company in order to play on the company's amateur basketball team. She was paid $75 for the job – thus retaining her amateur status – and excelled on the court, earning Amateur Athletic Union honours from 1930 to 1932.

In 1930 she tried her hand at athletics and won four events in an AAU competition. Two years later, at the AAU championships – which doubled as the Los Angeles 1932 Olympic Games qualifying competition – she earned Olympic qualification single-handedly. The sole representative from her company, Didrikson scored 30 points, eight more than the 22-person team that finished second. Across three hours, she took part in eight out of ten events, won five and set new world records in the javelin, 80m hurdles, high jump and baseball throw.

At the 1932 Los Angeles Olympic Games, Didrikson won two gold medals and a silver, with women only able to compete in three events. She won the javelin gold, set a world record of 11.7 seconds winning the 80m hurdles and finished second to Jean Smiley

in the high jump, this after her final jump was disallowed because of improper technique.

Didrikson picked up golf in 1935 and won that year's Texas Women's Amateur event, but the US Golf Association stripped her of her amateur status because she had competed professionally in other sports.

Unperturbed, in January 1938 she took part in the Los Angeles Open, a Professional Golfers' Association-run tournament. It would be 60 years before women again competed against men on the course. At that LA Open, she met professional wrestler George Zaharias and they were married in 1939, George becoming Babe's business manager and advisor.

Zaharias was not permitted to play golf as an amateur for 10 years, during which time she bowled and played tennis, expanding her sporting world.

The Associated Press named Zaharias their Female Athlete of the Year every year from 1945 to 1947 – she won six awards overall between 1932 and 1954, more than any other athlete, male or female – as she dominated the golf circuit, winning 17 of 18 tournaments before turning professional. The titles included becoming the first American to win both the US Women's Amateur and British Ladies Amateur. In 1948 she won her first US Women's Open, the World Championship and the All-American Open. She was a founding member of the Ladies Professional Golf Association and had a tournament named after her in her hometown of Beaumont, Texas, the Babe Zaharias Open. By 1950 she had collected every golf title available to her and completed the Grand Slam by winning the US Open, the Titleholders Championship and the Women's Western Open. She would win a total of 82 tournaments as an amateur or professional.

"ALL OF MY LIFE I HAVE ALWAYS HAD THE URGE TO DO THINGS BETTER THAN ANYBODY ELSE."

Babe Didrikson Zaharias

"She is beyond all belief until you see her perform," said sportswriter Grantland Rice. "Then you finally understand that you are looking at the most flawless section of muscle harmony, of complete mental and physical coordination, the world of sport has ever seen."

After the breakdown of her marriage, Zaharias began a relationship with fellow golfer Betty Dodd. "As Zaharias' marriage grew increasingly troubled, she spent more time with Dodd," Susan Cayleff wrote in her biography of the athlete, titled *Babe*. "The women toured together on the golf circuit, and eventually Dodd moved in with George and Babe for the last six years of Mildred's life. They never used the word 'lesbian' to describe their relationship, but there is little doubt that their relationship was both sexual and romantic and Didrikson has been described as the first lesbian gold medallist in Olympic athletics."

In 1953, Zaharias was diagnosed with colon cancer but she made her comeback one month after surgery. While wearing a colostomy bag, she won the Vare Trophy and a 10th and final US Women's Open championship title.

Her colon cancer returned in 1955, but she still played in eight events that season and won her final two tournaments. She died aged 45, while still one of the highest ranked players in women's golf.

FANNY BLANKERS-KOEN

The four gold medals that Dutch athlete Fanny Blankers-Koen won at the 1948 London Olympic Games made her the most successful athlete at the event. She matched the historic four gold medals won by Jesse Owens – whose signature she cherished – at the Berlin 1936 Games, and it made her the most successful female track athlete in a single Olympics.

More than sporting records, however, Blankers-Koen challenged the perception of mothers and defied the likes of British athletics team manager and BBC commentator Jack Crump, who said that the 30-year-old was "too old to make the grade".

Blankers-Koen had given birth to Jan Junior in 1942 and Fanneke in 1945 when she travelled to London in 1948, and she was criticized for stepping outside of the home.

"I got very many bad letters, people writing that I must stay home with my children and that I should not be allowed to run on a track with – how do you say it? – short trousers," she told the *New York Times* in 1982. "But I was a good mother. I had no time for much besides my house chores and training, and when I went shopping it was only to buy food for the family and never to buy dresses.

"One newspaperman wrote that I was too old to run, that I should stay at home and take care of my children. When I got to London, I

pointed my finger at him and I said: 'I show you.'"

She did. She won the 100m in a world-record equalling 11.5 seconds, finishing three seconds ahead of Great Britain's Dorothy Manley.

After sprinting to her first Olympic gold, she wanted to step back and said that she was missing her children. She told her husband and coach, Jan Blankers: "I am an Olympic champion and I don't want to run any more."

He didn't heed her request, instead encouraging her to sleep ahead of the 80m hurdles heats the following day.

She flew through the heats but the final was a different beast. "Nobody could have felt less like a champion," she said. "My knees trembled. I hit the fifth hurdle, my style went to pieces and I staggered home like a drunkard." Nonetheless, she leaned ahead of Great Britain's Maureen Gardner, just.

"I just leaned forward enough to get in front of Maureen," she told the *Sunday Times*. "I leaned so low, the tape cut my neck and the blood trickled on to my vest."

Once again, she tried to throw in the towel. Two golds were plenty. "You can go home if you wish," her husband said to the sobbing athlete before the 200m. "But in time you will be sorry. Just go out there and try to make the final, that will be enough."

Another final, another gold. This time she beat Great Britain's Audrey Williamson by 0.7 seconds. Her final gold medal came in the 4 x 100m relay.

In the final, Xenia Stad-de Jong led off for the Dutch and she was followed by Nettie Witziers-Timmer and Gerda van der Kade-Koudijs. When Blankers-Koen took the baton, the Netherlands sat in fourth place, narrowly behind Australia's Joyce King. "I thought to myself I could never win this, never, never, never. Then with 50m to go, I thought: 'Maybe I have a chance.' I ran faster than I have ever run,

"ALL I'VE DONE IS RUN FAST. I DON'T SEE WHY PEOPLE SHOULD MAKE MUCH FUSS ABOUT THAT."

Fanny Blankers-Koens

getting closer all the time, until a couple of metres from the line, I went into the lead."

It could have been more. Blankers-Koen was the world record holder in the high jump and long jump going into the tournament, but the Games only allowed track and field athletes to compete in a maximum of three individual events.

There were a number of other metaphorical hurdles for everyone at the London 1948 Games to clear. Following the end of World War Two, Germany and Japan were excluded, while the Soviet Union chose not to take part. Crippling austerity measures in Britain meant these were the austerity Games, with athletes having to bring their own food and travel to venues themselves. Blankers-Koen took the train to Wembley to compete.

She returned to the Netherlands a hero. Nicknamed "the flying housewife" and "the flying Dutchmam" on her arrival back home, she was praised by Queen Juliana, was made a Knight of the Order of Orange Nassau and was gifted a bike by the city of Amsterdam, her home town.

As well as her four Olympic titles she picked up five European titles, 58 Dutch championships, and set or tied 12 world records. In 1999 she was voted the Female Athlete of the Century by the International Association of Athletics Federations. She died, aged 85, in January 2004.

ALTHEA GIBSON

"The question I'm most frequently expected to answer is whether Althea Gibson will be permitted to play in the nationals this year," wrote former world number one and 18-time Grand Slam winner Alice Marble in *American Lawn Tennis* magazine in 1950.

"When I directed the question to a committee member of longstanding, he answered in the negative: 'Miss Gibson will not be permitted to play and it will be the reluctant duty of the committee to reject her entry.'

"I think it is time we faced a few facts. If tennis is a game for ladies and gentlemen, it is time we acted a little more like gentle people and less like sanctimonious hypocrites.

"The entrance of Negroes into national tennis is as inevitable as it has proven in baseball, in [American] football, or in boxing; there is no denying so much talent. The committee at Forest Hills has the power to stifle the efforts of one Althea Gibson, who may or may not be succeeded by others of her race who have equal or superior ability. They will knock at the door as she has done. Eventually, the tennis world will rise up en masse to protest the injustices perpetrated by our policymakers. Eventually – why not now?"

In 1950 segregation was still very much a reality for African-Americans. The Civil Rights movement was building, but the call for Althea Gibson to be permitted to play top tennis in the US came before Rosa Parks refused to give up her seat at the front of a segregated bus to a white person (in 1955), before Martin Luther King Jr's "I have a dream" speech (1963), before the assassination of Malcolm X (1965), and before the Civil Rights Act (1968).

The rules of the US Tennis Association prohibited racial or ethnic discrimination, but with players qualifying for the premier competition through sanctioned tournaments primarily held at white-only tennis clubs, they were banned in all but name.

Lobbying from the American Tennis Association (the oldest African-American sports organization in the US), the pressure from Marble and the prodigious talent of Gibson forced the hand of the USTA to extend an invitation to the National Championship (now the US Open) at Forest Hills and Gibson made history when she stepped onto the court, with racist abuse raining down from the stands, to suffer an extremely narrow defeat to the reigning Wimbledon champion Louise Brough in a storm-affected match.

Born in August 1927 in South Carolina to parents Daniel and Annie Bell Gibson, who worked as sharecroppers on a cotton farm, Gibson and her family moved to Harlem in 1930 with the Depression hitting the rural South hard. It was on the streets of Harlem, specifically 143rd Street, where they lived, that Gibson's talent with a racquet was uncovered. The street would be cordoned off in the daytime so kids could play and Gibson took up paddle tennis. By the age of 12 she was New York City's women's paddle tennis champion.

She was invited to join the Cosmopolitan Tennis Club as a junior member by Buddy Walker, a bandleader at a Harlem bar who ran the playstreet. The club was comprized mainly of African-American professional players and she was introduced to the Harlem River tennis courts. She wasn't that interested. At 13, she ditched school to street fight, play basketball and watch films.

She won her first ATA tournament in 1942 and eventually caught the eye of doctors Hubert Eaton (civil rights activist and tennis player) and Robert Johnson (ATA junior development programme founder, who would later mentor Arthur Ashe). They were leading the ATA's search for a player who could disrupt the USTA's all-white tournaments. They would invite her to live in their homes and coached her. She competed and won the ATA girls' division in 1944 and 1945, then played in the women's competition, losing the final in 1946 before winning her first of 10 straight titles the following year.

At the 1956 French Open (then the French Championships) she became the first African-American to win a Grand Slam. The following year she won both Wimbledon (singles and doubles, with Jewish British player Angela Buxton) and the National Championship. After the last of these titles, she was received a ticker-tape parade in New York. In her career, Gibson won a total of 11 Grand Slam titles, five singles, five doubles and one mixed doubles.

Aged 37, she swapped sports and became the first African-American woman to join the Ladies Professional Golf Tour. She spent 14 years on the Tour, breaking some course records in individual rounds, but she never finished better than 27th in a tournament, probably because she joined the Tour so late.

Often compared to Jackie Robinson, who became the first African-American to play Major League Baseball in 1947, Gibson shied away from being labelled as a pioneer. "I have never regarded myself as a crusader," she wrote in her autobiography. "I don't consciously beat the drums for any cause, not even the negro in the United States."

Whether she consciously beat the drum is irrelevant. Just by playing and winning, she pushed through barrier after barrier.

Bob Ryland, a former coach of Venus and Serena Williams, called her "one of the greatest players who ever lived".

He added: "Martina Navratilova couldn't touch her. I think she'd beat the Williams sisters."

Venus Williams said in 2003: "I am honoured to have followed in such great footsteps. Her accomplishments set the stage for my success, and through players like myself and Serena and many others to come, her legacy will live on."

KATHRINE SWITZER

The image is iconic. On April 19, 1967, after much preparation and having had to first convince her coach, Arnie Briggs, that she was up to it, Kathrine Switzer was running in the Boston Marathon.

S he was flanked by her boyfriend Tom Miller, then 15-time Boston Marathon veteran Briggs and friend John Leonard from Syracuse University's cross country team, where Switzer studied journalism. No woman had been recorded as having run in a marathon before. Briggs was only on board after she had run 26.2 miles with him. After they had reached the marker, she was ready to run an extra five miles and, at the end of 31 miles, Briggs hugged her before passing out. The next day he got her to sign up. She entered herself as K. V. Switzer and paid the $3 entry fee.

During the race heads turned but the response was overwhelmingly positive from fellow runners. "Hey! You gonna go the whole way?" "Gosh, it's great to see a girl here!" "Can you give me some tips to get my wife to run? She'd love it if I can just get her started," Switzer remembers in her autobiography, *Marathon Woman*.

Race manager Jock Semple had other ideas though. "[At the mile four marker] I heard the scraping noise of leather shoes coming up fast behind me, an alien and alarming sound amid the muted thump thumping of rubber-soled running shoes," says Switzer in her memoir. "Instinctively I jerked my head around quickly and looked square into the most vicious face

I'd ever seen. A big man, a huge man, with bared teeth was set to pounce, and before I could react he grabbed my shoulder and flung me back, screaming: 'Get the hell out of my race and give me those numbers!' Then he swiped down my front, trying to rip off my bib number, just as I leapt backward from him. He missed the numbers, but I was so surprised and frightened that I slightly wet my pants and turned to run. But now the man had the back of my shirt and was swiping at the bib number on my back. I was making little cries of aa-uh, aa-uh, not thinking at all, just trying to get away, when I saw tiny brave Arnie bat at him and try to push him away, shouting, 'Leave her alone, Jock. I've trained her, she's okay, leave her alone!'"

Cameras were clicking and her team came to help. Miller body-checked Semple, sending him flying into the air, then they ran hard.

"Everyone was shouting. I could hear the journalists on the truck behind us yelling, 'Go after her, go after her!' to the driver. The driver accelerated, popped the clutch, and I heard the truck buck and what unfortunately sounded like photographers, tripods, and crank cameras crashing down in a cursing melee…

"I wondered if I should step off the course. I did not want to mess up this prestigious race. But the thought was only a flicker. I knew if I quit, nobody would ever believe that women had the capability to run 26-plus miles. If I quit, everybody would say it was a publicity stunt. If I quit, it would set women's sports back, way back, instead of forward. If I quit, I'd never run Boston. If I quit, Jock Semple and all those like him would win. My fear and humiliation turned to anger."

The race was far from over, Semple caught up with them on a bus and shouted warnings. Then, Miller accused the shaken and desperate to finish Switzer, of having jeopardized his chances of competing in the Olympics.

"I've hit an official, and now I'll get kicked out of the AAU," he told

"IF I QUIT, IT WOULD SET WOMEN'S SPORTS BACK, WAY BACK, INSTEAD OF FORWARD"

Kathrine Switzer

her. "I didn't hit the official, you hit the official, Tom," she replied. Miller ripped off his numbers and disappeared into a crowd of runners.

Having pushed through the tears and reached the midway point, they saw Miller walking and begged her to walk with him.

"I can't, Tom, as slow as I'm going, I've got some momentum here," she replied as they passed.

Eventually she stumbled across the finish line, having run the whole way with Briggs and Leonard by her side.

During the final miles she reflected on what her competing meant. "I wondered why other women didn't run, thinking that they just didn't get it. Wait a minute, maybe they believed all those old myths like running ruins your reproductive organs, and it scared them away because they didn't know better and nobody gave them opportunities to disprove this nonsense.

"My folks and Arnie had given me this chance, and it dawned on me that I was not special after all; just lucky. My thinking rolled on: The reason there are no intercollegiate sports for women at big universities, no scholarships, prize money, or any races longer than 800 meters is because women don't have the opportunities to prove they want those things. If they could just take part, they'd feel the power and accomplishment and the situation would change. After what happened today, I felt responsible to create those opportunities. I felt elated, like I'd made a great discovery. In fact, I had."

It would be 17 years before the women's marathon was included in the Olympic Games. The first winner, at Los Angeles 1984, was an American, Joan Benoit, who had been nine years old when Switzer ran in Boston on Patriots Day 1967.

PAT GREGORY

The history of women's football is rich and deep. Women playing football can be traced back to the origins of the sport itself, in China, where there is evidence that an early ball game, Cuju, was also occasionally played by women. The game has come a long way since then but, in England, women's football faced a huge setback in 1921, when a Football Association ban scythed it down at a time it was generating mass attendances.

For Patricia Gregory, who fell in love with the double-winning heroes of Bill Nicholson's Tottenham men's team in the 1960s, the absence of women in the game was evident early on.

"My father didn't want to take me to White Hart Lane because he didn't think it was a place for women," she told *Women in Football*. "I quite understood when I went, because of the behaviour of some of the men.

"My father and I went down to Tottenham Town Hall to see them bring the cup back [in 1967 when they won the FA Cup and Gregory was 19]. I remember looking up at them on a balcony and thinking, 'why don't girls play football?'"

That spurred Gregory into action. She got in touch with the *Hornsey Journal* and before long, girls were writing in, wanting to join a team that didn't yet exist.

"MY FATHER DIDN'T WANT TO TAKE ME TO WHITE HART LANE BECAUSE HE DIDN'T THINK IT WAS A PLACE FOR WOMEN."

Pat Gregory

Gregory founded White Ribbon FC from a meeting of 15 girls in the sitting room of her parents' house but they immediately came up against a ban that Gregory didn't know existed. They had written to the local council about hiring a pitch and training facilities "only to discover the 1921 rule existed," she told the *I* newspaper. "The council wrote back and said we weren't allowed to hire either of them. This was the first indication it wasn't as simple as we thought."

So, she wrote to the paper again explaining the problem and a men's team called White Star offered their facilities. Without teams to play against, Gregory got in touch with the FA, but was referred back to the 1921 decision of the governing body.

"I enclose herewith for your information a copy of the Council decision of December, 1921, which decision was confirmed by the Council in December, 1962," the reply from FA secretary Denis Follows, dated July 21, 1967, said. "As the Football Association does not recognize ladies football teams, I am unable to inform you of any League to which you could apply for Membership."

The ban read: "Complaints having been made as to football being played by women, Council felt impelled to express the strong opinion that the game of football is quite unsuitable for females and should not be encouraged.

"Complaints have also been made as to the conditions under which some of the matches have been arranged and played, and the appropriation of receipts to other than charitable objects. The Council are further of the opinion that an excessive proportion of the receipts are absorbed in expenses and an inadequate percentage devoted to charitable objects. For these reasons the Council requests the Clubs belonging to the Association refuse the use of their grounds for such matches."

White Ribbon was not the best team by all accounts, but they were having fun and the team travelled around playing youth teams. Eventually,

"AS THE FOOTBALL ASSOCIATION DOES NOT RECOGNIZE LADIES FOOTBALL TEAMS, I AM UNABLE TO INFORM YOU OF ANY LEAGUE TO WHICH YOU COULD APPLY FOR MEMBERSHIP."

Denis Follows, FA Secretary

Gregory was connected with Arthur Hobbs, who was championing women's football in south-east England.

Facing barrier after barrier, in 1969 Gregory, Hobbs and others, with 44 clubs represented, founded the Women's FA and established the first Women's FA Cup, which was played in 1971. Six months after the first meeting, seven regional leagues attended the first annual general meeting of the new Women's Football Association – the South East, Kent, the Midlands, Sussex, West Mercia, Northampton and Southampton.

Momentum was with the WFA, which was run voluntarily, and at the end of 1969 Follows wrote to the WFA stating that the FA had agreed to "rescind the council's resolution of 1921".

"There was no flash of light or anything like that," Gregory told the *Daily Telegraph* in 2021. "I wish I could tell you there was great excitement, but there wasn't. We just solved each problem as it came, one by one."

In 1972 the first England women's game was played, but it was not until 1993 that the WFA was merged into the FA.

CHERYL WHITE

On June 15, 1971, at Thistledown racetrack in North Randall, Ohio, 17-year-old Cheryl White became the first licensed Black female jockey when she crossed the finish line, in last place, in a six-furlong – 1,320 yards (1,207 metres) race for maidens (horses which had never won).

A few years later, she recounted the moment she shot into the record books on Ace Reward. "I just wanted those gates to open," she told a journalist for *BetChicago*.

White followed in the footsteps of a trail blazed by Eliza Carpenter 64 years earlier. Carpenter, who was born into slavery in 1851 on a Virginia plantation, was sold twice before the end of the American Civil War. After the conclusion of the war in 1865, Carpenter moved to Kentucky, where she took an interest in thoroughbred horses and began to ride and learn the trade. Black jockeys were not unheard of, in fact, 13 of the first 25 editions of the Kentucky Derby – America's most famous race – were won by African-American men, but women jockeys of any race were not permitted to ride.

Carpenter was more than a jockey. In 1893, aged 44, she took part in the largest land run in American history, the Cherokee Strip Land run, which allowed the participants, if they could get there first, to claim one of 42,000 pieces of Indian Territory that had been bought by the government after it had banned use of the land for cattle grazing. The boom of a cannon began the run, and Carpenter – riding her chestnut mare – was

among the 100,000 to set off. The duo covered the 12 miles of the Run in 45 minutes to reach a good site where she could train thoroughbred and quarter horses. It made her the only Black stable owner in Oklahoma, and one of very few African-American racehorse owners, while still racing herself too.

Despite leading the way, it wasn't until 1939, 15 years after Carpenter's death, that Anna Lee Aldred would become the first American woman to receive a professional jockey's licence, albeit in Mexico. In 1968 a court demanded the Maryland Racing Commission grant a licence to Kathryn Kusner, making her the first woman in the United States to have a jockey's licence. Unfortunately, she was injured, so her replacement, Barbara Jo Ruben, became the first licenced woman jockey to start a race. Then, in 1971, came White.

White's father was an owner and trainer himself, Raymond White, who ran two horses in the Kentucky Derby. Her mother, Doris, also owned racehorses and it was riding her mother's horses where White's talent was noticed.

Her debut at Thistledown drew national attention and she graced the cover of African-American magazine JET in July 1971. "Winsome Cheryl White, JET's cover girl (July 29), became the first Black woman jockey in American thoroughbred racing history to win a race," the magazine stated.

"Miss White, in a recent interview, told JET: 'I plan on furthering my education. I could fall off tonight and be set up for life … I want to teach … I want something to fall back on.'

"For now, it's up at 6 a.m. for the racer who gets $35 every time she mounts a horse in a race and will pocket 10 percent of her horse's earnings each time she places first."

It is believed that White won more than 750 races and earned over $762,000 in a career spanning 21 years. As a thoroughbred rider, she became the first woman to secure two race wins on the same day in

"SHE JUST DID HER THING... I DON'T KNOW THAT SHE UNDERSTOOD HER SIGNIFICANCE, OR PLACE IN HISTORY."

Raymond White Jr, Cheryl White's brother

two different states when she rode a winner at Thistledown, Ohio, and then at Waterford Park – now Mountaineer Park – in West Virginia in 1971. In 1983 she broke another record by becoming the first female jockey to win five races in one day, at Fresno Fair in California.

"The last winner I rode that day was Montfort, a 10-year-old, and making his 100th start," she laughed, in conversation with Tina Hines in 2007.

As a rider of Appaloosa horses, she was the first woman to win the Appaloosa Horse Club's Jockey of the Year award in 1977 and would win it a further three times in 1983, 1984 and 1985.

In the early 1990s White stepped away from the saddle, bar competing in a few Lady Legends events, and would become the first woman to serve as a racing official after passing the California Horse Racing Board's Steward Examination.

White was a member of the Appaloosa Hall of Fame, inducted in 2001, and a recipient of the African-American Sports Hall of Fame's Award of Merit.

She died in 2019, aged 65. "Cheryl was never a great self-promoter, and wasn't concerned with the politics of racing," said Raymond White Jr, her brother, in a press release announcing her death. "She just did her thing. She didn't understand what she had accomplished. I don't know that she understood her significance, or place in history."

MIA HAMM

"The vision of a champion is someone who is bent over, drenched in sweat, at the point of exhaustion when no one else is watching." Those were the words that the most successful college football coach in history, Anson Dorrance, of the University of North Carolina, scribbled on some paper before handing it to Mia Hamm. Dorrance had been driving to the Chapel Hill campus and seen his star senior running drills alone in the park.

Hamm had arrived in North Carolina in 1989 as a 17-year-old with a growing reputation. At 15 she had been the youngest player ever to play for the US women's national team. In 1991, still the youngest player on the team, she competed in the first official FIFA Women's World Cup, where the United States, with Dorrance as coach, charged to its first World Cup. In the first game, Hamm scored the winner to give the US a 3–2 win over Sweden and she also scored in the team's 5–0 group stage defeat of Brazil.

Dorrance, who was Hamm's guardian in her freshman year at North Carolina as her parents were living abroad, was the brains behind the winning mentality that set the US women's national team apart from the rest. UNC women's team coach since 1979, he has fed a whole host of players through his intense college programme into every US World Cup-winning side since.

Hamm thrived under his tutelage. "I grew up always good at sports, but being a girl, I was never allowed to feel as good about it as guys were," she said. "My toughness wasn't celebrated. But then I got to the University of North Carolina, and it was OK to want to be the best."

It was Hamm's desire to be the best, an insatiable desire, that drove her

to the top. Her second World Cup, in 1995, ended less favourably, with the team knocked out by Norway at the semi-final stage, but the magic player would score the second goal in a 2–0 defeat of China in the third-place play-off.

The 1999 Women's World Cup in the US catapulted the US team into the spotlight and Hamm to superstardom, making her arguably the first women's football poster-girl to transcend the sport. The US's profile ahead of the tournament had been boosted by gold medal success at the Atlanta Olympics in 1996 and in the build-up to the World Cup, Hamm broke the all-time international goalscoring record when she fired in her 108th goal, against Brazil, in Orlando.

A month later, Hamm scored goal 110 and provided an assist for Julie Foudy in a 3–0 opening World Cup victory over Denmark. By the time the final rocked around, America had fully embraced the team that had returned to little fanfare after winning the 1991 competition. The Rose Bowl in Pasadena, California, was packed with a crowd of 90,185, until March 2022 the all-time world record attendance for a women's football match.

Hamm's star was sky-high. Nike named its largest building on its campus after her, while in 2012 Forbes labelled her the "most marketable female soccer player ever" for the millions generated from endorsements. She signed deals with Gatorade, Nike, Dreyer's ice cream, Pepsi, Nabisco, Fleet Bank, Earthgrains and Powerbar. Her face adorned Wheaties boxes, Mattel produced a Mia Hamm Barbie and, in 2000, Nintendo released the video game Mia Hamm Soccer 64 for the Nintendo 64. She also did interviews everywhere and anywhere. The attention did not come naturally, but Hamm understood the wider impact being visible could have.

"It's her refreshingly sincere selflessness – in everything she does – that helped make her an icon," Julie Foudy wrote for espnW.com in 2012. "The irony of it all, of course, is that Mia never wanted the attention. She just wanted to play. And she wanted to win. I mean, she REALLY wanted to win. When she was thrust into the spotlight in the late 1990s, she could have easily declined interviews, refused photo shoots, shied away from the media. Instead, and intuitively, without anyone ever telling her what had to be done, Mia understood that women's soccer needed attention.

"She understood that girls needed to see other girls playing sports. She understood that the popularity of soccer rested almost squarely upon her shoulders. Most of all, and perhaps most important to our team's success, she understood that it was about the group, not about her."

In 2004 Hamm was one of two women, with former teammate Michelle Akers, named on Pelé's list of the top 125 living football players. In 2012 she was named the Greatest Female Athlete of the Last 40 Years by ESPN.

"It was a bit overwhelming because there are so many great female athletes that I've looked up to and both watched compete and played alongside," she told *Forbes*. "It was overwhelming to be considered at the top of all these athletes I thought so much of when there is Billy [Billie] Jean King, Chris Evert and Jackie Joyner-Kersee. For me, it was Michelle Akers."

The US failed to defend their World Cup title in 2003, losing to eventual winners Germany at the semi-final stage. The Athens 2004 Olympics Games saw Hamm retire from football on a huge high. She had set the record for the most international goals scored by anyone in the world, male or female, 158 – a record which stood until 2013, when Abby Wambach passed it (Wambach's tally was overtaken by Canada's Christine Sinclair in 2020). In Athens, Hamm provided the assist for Heather O'Reilly that gave the US a 2–1 semi-final extra-time victory over Germany and the US defeated Brazil 2–1 after extra time in the gold medal match.

Following the death of her adopted brother Garrett in 1997 from a rare blood disease, Hamm founded the Mia Hamm Foundation to raise awareness. She is a global ambassador for FC Barcelona, a co-owner of NWSL side Angel City FC and is on the board of directors of AS Roma.

BILLIE JEAN KING

In 1973, the US Open Tennis Championships became the first major sports tournament to award equal prize money to men and women. It is no accident that half, and four of the top five, of the women on the Forbes list of the 10 highest-paid female athletes in 2022 were tennis players.

In order, Naomi Osaka, Serena Williams, Venus Williams, Garbiñe Muguruza and Ash Barty filled positions one, two, three, five and eight. Back in 2017, that number was eight of 10. Further proof of women's place in tennis came when Emma Raducanu's 2021 US Open final defeat of Leylah Fernandez drew a bigger television audience than the men's final between Novak Djokovic and Daniil Medvedev the following day, with a peak audience of 3.4m viewers to 2.7m on ESPN.

These were not organic developments. The fact that it is only now, in the 2020s, that other sports are feeling the pressure to distribute equal prize money for major competitions or that their top stars are starting to earn big – with the Forbes top 10 completed by gymnastics legend Simone Biles, golf duo Jin Young Ko and Nelly Korda, India's badminton star PV Sindhu and basketball's Candace Parker – reflects just how far ahead of the curve tennis has been.

Leading the charge for equality in tennis, and equality in sport generally, was and is Billie Jean King. King was born in 1943 into a sporty, working-class family. Her father was a firefighter and had played baseball, basketball and track athletics, while her mother was a housewife and an excellent swimmer. Her younger brother, Randy Moffitt, would play Major League Baseball

as a pitcher for the San Francisco Giants, Houston Astros and Toronto Blue Jays. King was a talented baseball and softball player and took up tennis at the age of 11, on the suggestion of her father. Her parents got her to save up to pay for her first racquet from pocket money earned from odd jobs.

She started lessons on the free public courts in Long Beach, California, and began building her wider game around a very aggressive playing style starting point. King was confronted with inequality throughout her tennis-playing life, from being excluded from a group picture at a tournament because she was wearing tennis shorts her mother had made her rather than a tennis dress to having to work two jobs while studying history at California State University because she could not get a sports scholarship. This was despite her having won a Wimbledon doubles title in 1961, aged 17. Meanwhile, former husband Larry King, whom she met at university and married in 1963, was studying on a full sports scholarship and played for one of the school's best men's teams.

From the 1950s to the 1970s, protest swept the US – in opposition to the Vietnam War, in support of gay rights, through the Civil Rights movement, and in support of women's rights. King and those around her were being shaped by this time. There was a growing clamour for professionalism, but the first open Grand Slam tournament (for amateurs and professionals) came only at the 1968 French Open.

By 1971 King had three Wimbledon singles wins (including the Open 1968 edition), one US Championship and one Australian Championship. A consummate doubles player, she had already claimed 11 women's Grand Slam doubles titles and seven mixed doubles too.

It was in 1971, three years after the Open era began, that King pushed for equal prize money in the men's and women's game. She threatened to boycott the 1973 US Open without equal prize money on offer, helping to force the change through (although pay parity was only rolled out in the Australian Open in 2001, the French Open in 2006 and Wimbledon in 2007). Her husband Larry would develop the idea for a professional tour for women and helped organize a group of players which would become known as the "Original Nine" and, with the backing of Gladys Heldman of *World Tennis* magazine and CEO of tobacco company Phillip Morris, Joe Cullman, the Virginia Slims pro circuit was started and as a result, the Women's Tennis Association was founded with King as its first president. In September of the same year, King played the famous "Battle of the Sexes" exhibition match with the 55-year-old former pro player and self-proclaimed "male chauvinist" Bobby Riggs. There was $100,000 at stake and, more importantly for King, "I thought it would set us back 50 years if I didn't win that match. It would ruin the women's tour and affect all women's self-esteem."

King won the match in straight sets, coming from behind in the first. The match drew an attendance of more than 30,000, and a global TV audience of around 90 million.

She would go on to win a further six Grand Slam singles titles, seven Grand Slam doubles titles and four Grand Slam mixed doubles tournaments and won a total of 129 singles titles across her career.

She was forced to acknowledge a same-sex relationship in 1981, when her former secretary exposed their relationship in a palimony case against Billie Jean and Larry. Nonetheless their marriage ended only in 1987 and they stayed close friends. Homophobic parents and the potential public backlash prevented King from embracing her sexuality, but she is now married to former doubles partner Ilana Kloss and is a vocal advocate for LGBTQ+ rights, having finally been able to talk with her parents about it at the age of 51.

King's women's sports legacy is deep and her unerring drive for equal pay in tennis has influenced and continues to influence fights for equality in the US and worldwide.

JUNKO TABEI

When the Fukushima-born Junko Tabei hiked the peaks of the volcano Mount Nasu with her class, a new world was opened to the diminutive 10-year-old. On the May 16, 1975, 25 years later, she would become the 36th person to climb Mount Everest and the first woman to do so – a moniker she rejected, saying: "I did not intend to be the first woman on Everest."

The journey to the top of the world's tallest peak was not straightforward. Born Junko Ishibashi in 1939, she, like many of her generation, grew up in a country crippled by the legacy of the Second World War and with the expectation that women belonged in the kitchen, keeping the home and raising children. With designs of becoming a teacher, she studied English and American Literature at university and became a member of the mountaineering club, where her passion was reignited. After graduating she joined more mountaineering clubs dominated by men and the reception she

"I DID NOT INTEND TO BE THE FIRST WOMAN ON EVEREST."

Junko Tabei

received was mixed, with the older generation welcoming her into the fold more readily than the younger. Her participation pushed against cultural and societal stereotypes and she challenged them further through her marriage to Masanobu Tabei, who she met during an ascent of Mount Tanigawa. Masanobu, who worked for Honda, took care of their two children while she went on expeditions. "Most Japanese men of my generation would expect the woman to stay at home and clean the house," she said in an interview later.

Tabei worked her way up from Japan's Mount Fuji to the Matterhorn and, in 1969, she founded the Joshi-Tohan women-only climbing club. Their belief was that women should be able to organize and lead their own expeditions and had a motto to that effect: "Let's go on an overseas expedition by ourselves."

Their first trip took place the following year, to Annapurna III in the Himalayas, the 42nd highest mountain in the world. With Sherpa support, the all-women team attempted a new route from the south, with the only ascent prior coming from the north. The 4'9" (1.45m) tall Tabei was one of four climbers to reach the summit.

Everest captured the pioneers' attentions next, but they had to contend with a four-year waiting list. While they waited, the group of 15 who made up the Japanese Women's Everest Expedition attempted to raise funds to cover the costs of the journey. Regularly told that the world's tallest peak was no place for women, the group eventually earned the backing of Japanese television company NTV at the eleventh hour and from the country's largest newspaper, *Yomiuri Shimbun*. During that time the team – which included teachers, a counsellor, a computer programmer and more – sewed their own sleeping bags and crafted things to sell in order to raise funds.

The group made it to Everest in the spring of 1975 and began working their way up the mountain. At 9,000 feet, they were engulfed by an avalanche while they were camped beneath the Lhotse face (a 1.125km wall of glacial blue ice). Tabei and others were buried, and she was knocked unconscious, but a team of Sherpas managed to free them.

The mountaineer was unable to walk for two days due to injuries suffered in the avalanche, but she reached the summit 12 days after the incident, crawling to the top on her hands and knees, with just her guide, before describing the summit as, "smaller than a tatami mat", and saying, "all I felt was relief", on finally reaching the top.

Tibetan labourer Phanthog became the second woman to reach the summit of Everest just 11 days later.

Tabei went on to complete the Seven Summits, scaling the highest mountain on each continent (Mount Everest, Mount Elbrus, Kilimanjaro, Puncak Jaya, Vinson, Denali and Aconcagua), completing the task in 1992, making her the first woman to do so, and climbed the tallest peaks in 70 countries before her death in 2016.

Her postgraduate studies in 2000 focused on the environmental degradation of Everest caused by heavy climber traffic and the waste left behind and she served as director of the Himalayan Adventure Trust of Japan.

"Everest has become too crowded. It needs a rest now," she said in 2003.

"EVEREST HAS BECOME TOO CROWDED. IT NEEDS A REST NOW."

Junko Tabei

NADIA
COMĂNECI

Nadia Comăneci was taken to gymnastics classes as a child because her mother, Stefania-Alexandrina, wanted to find a release for her daughter's boundless energy. She began lessons when at nursery in Romania, with a local team called Flacăra, "The Flame".

At the age of six, Nadia was spotted practising cartwheels in the playground of her primary school by former junior boxing champion and national hammer-throwing champion Béla Károlyi. He recruited the young gymnast to his boarding-school style gym, run by himself and his wife Márta, though she was able to live at home for a number of years. It was a tough life for these young gymnasts, according to Nadia's contemporaries.

Emelia Eberle – who now goes by the name of Trudi Kollar – who joined the gym in 1976, spoke to the *Guardian* in 2008 and said the regime was "brutal". "Nobody's perfect, so obviously we did mistakes. And we, you know, just got smacked everywhere from Béla – on all our body parts. He has huge hands and it hurts," she said. Rodica Dunca, another gymnast, told *ProSport* magazine in 2002: "On certain days we were hit until blood was pouring out of our noses. You can say it was a concentration camp, or even a prison." While Ecaterina Szabo said that after the Károlyis defected to the United States in 1981: "I was so happy that I'd escaped them. I'll never forget the slaps in the face and the beatings I got from Béla Károlyi."

Károlyi has always denied the allegations against him.

In 1970, aged nine, Comăneci began competing and became the youngest-ever gymnast to win the Romanian Nationals. The following year she competed in her first international competition, a junior meet

between Romania and then Yugoslavia, where she won her first all-around title and helped her nation to a team gold.

Her first major success came in 1975, aged 13 years old. At the European Women's Artistic Gymnastics Championships, at Skien in Norway, Comăneci won all-around gold and golds in all events but the floor exercise. That year, she became the youngest-ever competitor at the International Champions All Tournament at Wembley. The *Guardian* reported: "At 13 years old Nadia Comăneci is still both physically too exuberant and spiritually too intense to be the perfect gymnast, but give her another year or two and there may be no confining the exquisite talent of this tiny Romanian girl."

At the Montreal Olympic Games in 1976, she did the unthinkable, achieving a "perfect 10" score on the uneven bars in the team event. It was so unthinkable that the scoreboard could only show "1.00" as it wasn't able to display a maximum score. It was just the beginning; the 14-year-old raked up another six perfect scores on her way to three gold medals in the all-around, uneven bars and balance beam disciplines.

"Everybody was surprised to see a 14-year-old being able to do the level of gymnastics that I did, but even I didn't know that I was extraordinary at the time," she said.

Sadly, all was not rosy for the new superstar. There was speculation that, in 1977, Comăneci had attempted to take her own life by drinking bleach. She denied the rumours until 1990 when, in *LIFE* magazine, she confirmed she had in fact tried to kill herself, saying she was hospitalized for two days and was "glad because I didn't have to go to the gym."

The young star battled with her changing body as she grew older but continued to compete. At the 1978 World Championships in

Strasbourg, she won a gold medal
on the beam and silvers in the vault
and in the team competition. The following
year, in Copenhagen, she won a third consecutive
European all-around title, the first gymnast, male or female, to do so. At
the Worlds in Fort Worth, USA, a metal grip buckle cut her wrist and she
got blood poisoning. Despite a hospital stay and minor surgery, against
the advice of doctors, she was determined to compete on the beam
and scored 9.95. At the 1980 Olympic Games in Moscow she won two
more gold medals, on the beam and floor.

Following a 1981 tour of the US, Béla and Márta Károlyi defected,
but Comăneci wanted to stay in Romania. The defection of her
coaches, and their choreographer, rattled the Romanian establishment
and fearing they could lose their biggest star, they clamped down on
her freedom.

After her retirement in 1984 the treatment got more brutal. "Life took
on a new bleakness," she said in her memoir. "I was cut off from making
the small amount of extra money that had really made a difference in
my family's life. It was also insulting that a normal person in Romania
had the chance to travel, whereas I could not … when my gymnastics
career was over, there was no longer any need to keep me happy. I was
to do as I was instructed, just as I'd done my entire life … If Béla hadn't
defected, I would still have been watched, but his defection brought a
spotlight on my life, and it was blinding. I started to feel like a prisoner."

A few weeks before the Romanian revolution in 1989, Comăneci
travelled, with others, across the border into Hungary before heading to
Austria and boarding a plane to the US.

She is now honorary president of the Romanian Gymnastics
Federation and of the Romanian Olympic Committee and runs an
academy with her husband, former US gymnast Bart Conner.

ANN BANCROFT

Ann Bancroft's first big adventure was not any of the expeditions that have put her into the record books but when her family, from Minnesota, uprooted everything to spend two years in Kenya when Bancroft was in the fifth and sixth grades.

" Kenya was pivotal for our whole family," she told *Uplifting Voices*. "We refer to it all the time. For me, it was watching my parents take a risk in taking us all and not knowing all the answers. Discovering. Also understanding that there is a world outside of our neighbourhood and state."

Bancroft struggled at school. She wanted to like it, but it was hard, and her dyslexia didn't help. She would eventually go on to graduate from the University of Oregon with a degree in physical education, but her youth was filled with outdoor adventures. Her father took her camping and on canoeing trips in the north of the state and, aged eight, she led her own mini expeditions, roping her cousins into winter camping trips in their backyard.

After university, Bancroft was a camper and staff member at the YMCA Camp Widjiwagan in Minnesota, where she taught, became a wilderness instructor and gym teacher. With an insatiable desire for adventure not placated, she left work after five years to join the "Will Steger International North Pole Expedition".

"I did the North Pole in 1986, with 7 men and 49 male dogs," she said in an interview with *Uplifting Voices*. "At that time, there were no GPS devices, so we navigated with sextant compass and wind and sun."

On arrival at the summit of the globe, Bancroft, then 30, became the first woman to do so on foot and dogsled as part of the first confirmed

trek to reach the North Pole without needing a resupply. The trip took 56 days and was riddled with setbacks: Bancroft fell through thin ice; a faulty stove set a tent alight; two serious injuries (Bob Mantell – frostbitten feet – and Bob McKerrow – broken ribs after being caught under a runaway sled – both having to be airlifted off the expedition); the loss of a lead dog, Critter (who struggled without Mantell); and their only means of navigation malfunctioned. Nevertheless, the team made it across 1,000 miles of shifting ice in temperatures that plummeted as low as –70 degrees Fahrenheit (–57°C).

Bancroft's journeying did not end there. In 1992 she led the first American women's east-to-west crossing of Greenland then, in 1993, she put together the first all-women expedition to the South Pole – named the American Women's Expedition to the South Pole. "They are very different places," she said of the Poles. "Challenging in different ways as a result. North Pole is travelled in early March to early May – spring in Northern Hemisphere. It is still very cold, –70°F in the beginning. Being on the ocean, even frozen there is a humidity which makes it very hard to feel dry even in sub-zero temps. Very challenging. Also the currents make the ice a shifting element. It can buckle up into huge mountains or separate with no way to cross.

"Antarctica is a continent covered with an icecap. Huge glacier. It is filled with deep crevices often obscured. We also pulled sleds ourselves with all our belongings rather than having dogs pull. The wind is a constant on a continent the size of the US and Mexico combined. We

"WE TRAVELLED FROM SEA LEVEL TO CLOSE TO 10,000 FEET."

Ann Bancroft

travelled from sea level to close to 10,000 feet. This makes for a chilly place, regardless of the fact we are travelling in summer."

Ahead of the trip, Bancroft had started up her own foundation, which produced curricula based on the expedition and reached more than 200,000 children.

In reaching the South Pole she became the first woman to cross both polar ice caps. In 2001 her name would be in the record books once more, alongside Norwegian explorer Liv Arnesen, this time for sailing and skiing across Antarctica's 1,717-mile (2,763km) landmass in 94 days. And, in 2005, she was inducted into the National Women's Hall of Fame for the US.

Bancroft's activities now target some of the biggest questions facing the globe. In 2017 she travelled 1,500 miles along the Ganges River to raise awareness of the importance of clean water, and sailed down the Mississippi River to highlight the same cause in 2018.

STEFFI GRAF

When Steffi Graf was three years old, her father Peter, a car and insurance salesman, began to teach her how to swing a wooden racket in the family's sitting room in their home in Brühl, using the sofa as a net.

If she rallied 25 shots, she would be rewarded with ice cream. "Most of the time," Peter Graf later told the *New York Times*, "on the 25th ball, I would hit it too hard or so she could not return it, because you cannot have ice cream all the time." By the age of four she was on a court learning the game of tennis and a year later she was competing in her first tournament. She was a professional at the age of 13, and soon rocketed into the public consciousness. When she was 16, she already had victories over the dominant duo of Chris Evert and Martina Navratilova, having lost six times to Evert and thrice to Navratilova. Graf's first Grand Slam, the 1987 French Open – a 6–4, 4–6, 8–6 final victory over Navratilova – came aged 17, and she became the world No. 1 as an 18-year-old. It had been a meteoric rise, fuelled by a work-rate moulded by her father, who took control of her schedule and commitments.

"NOBODY IN THE WORLD CAN DO WHAT SHE DOES."

Zina Garrison

In 1988 she defeated Evert in the Australian Open final without dropping a set, defended her French Open title against Natasha Zvereva, ended Navratilova's run of six straight titles at Wimbledon by coming from 5–7, 0–2 down to the reigning champion to win 5–7, 6–2, 6–1, and she beat Gabriela Sabatini at the US Open. By winning the Australian Open, French Open, Wimbledon and US Open finals, Graf became the first player in history to win 28 Grand Slam singles matches in a single year. Less than two weeks later, she was competing at the Seoul Olympics, where her gold medal gave her what is now nicknamed the Golden Slam. It was the first time for 64 years that tennis had been an Olympic medal sport – and Graf had won the exhibition tournament at Los Angeles in 1984. "I came here really tired," she told the *New York Times* of the Olympics. "I was not expecting too much of myself.

"I am excited because I played great tennis. I am very pleased, especially after the last couple of days when I did not play that well."

In total, Graf won a total of 107 singles titles, including 22 Grand Slam singles titles, and was ranked No. 1 in the world for a record 377 weeks. In one spell between 1989 and 1990, she won 11 straight tournaments.

Graf ushered in a new era, setting the stage for the big hitters of tennis such as Monica Seles and Venus and Serena Williams.

"Nobody in the world can do what she does," said Zina Garrison in 1989 of Graf's devastating forehand range. "Her forehand puts fear in everybody."

Many cite Graf as one of the greatest tennis players of all time. In 1999 she was named the Greatest Female Tennis Player of the 20th

"HER FOREHAND PUTS FEAR IN EVERYBODY."

Zina Garrison

Century by an Associated Press panel. In 2012 the Tennis Channel put her at the top of its list of the 100 Greatest Players of All Time. In 2018 Tennis.com ran a poll of readers to find the Greatest Ever Women's Tennis Player, which Graf topped. A similar poll in the *Guardian* in 2020 saw Graf come first when readers were asked who they rated the greatest female tennis player of the past 50 years.

Despite the constant praise, Graf is modest. "Let other people be the judge of that," she replied to the *New York Times* when asked about her place in history on her retirement in 1999.

Instead, she has deflected the attention onto Navratilova. "For me, she is the uncontested No. 1; she has left a mark on the sport like no one else," she told the German news agency DPA.

"It's kind of her to say that," Navratilova said in reply to the *New York Times*. "But I don't see how you can really come out and say point-blank who's the greatest. When I first started out, I wanted to be No. 1, and then I wanted to be the greatest of all time, but the closer I got, I realised it was a bunch of baloney."

Billie Jean King was more emphatic: "Steffi is definitely the greatest women's tennis player of all time."

It should be said these comments all came before Serena Williams' long period of domination.

HASSIBA BOULMERKA

"That year I didn't run a single race in Algeria, it was simply too risky. I could have been killed at any moment."

Hassiba Boulmerka's preparations for the 1992 Barcelona Olympic Games were not ideal. Born in Constantine, in the north-east of Algeria, she began running at the age of 10 and began collecting medals at regional, national and international levels at 800m and 1,500m.

Her first big title came in 1991 when she won the 800m race at the Golden Gala meet in Rome. One month later, she won the 1,500m final at the Tokyo World Championships. It made her the first African woman to win a World Athletics Championship gold medal.

She was greeted by thousands of fans on her return and was escorted with fellow athlete Noureddine Morceli through the capital Algiers in a car with the top down. But her success was against a backdrop of turmoil in the country. The cancellation of parliamentary elections in early 1992, after the Islamic Salvation Front appeared to have beaten the ruling National Liberation Front, sparked a civil war during which 250,000 died. The high-profile Boulmerka became a

"THAT YEAR I DIDN'T RUN A SINGLE RACE IN ALGERIA... I COULD HAVE BEEN KILLED AT ANY MOMENT."

Hassiba Boulmerka

target, including death threats, to her and her family. It forced her to move to Berlin via train.

"I remember it well," she told the BBC. "It was Friday prayers at our local mosque, and the Imam said that I was not a Muslim, because I had run in shorts, shown my arms and my legs. He said I was anti-Muslim."

Ahead of the 1992 Olympics all communication with her family was cut off after the central telegraph office in her hometown had its lines severed.

Boulmerka travelled to Barcelona to compete while the war raged back home and armed guards travelled with her to the stadium. "They even came with me to the bathroom," she said.

On August 8, Boulmerka bided her time behind rival Lyudmila Rogacheva before accelerating past her with 200m to go. She was emphatic in the significance of her victory. "As I crossed the line, I thrust a fist into the air," Boulmerka told the BBC. "It was a symbol of victory, of defiance. It was to say: 'I did it! I won! And now, if you kill me, it'll be too late. I've made history!'

"I tried to hold myself together, to be brave, but the tears just started to fall [on the podium]. They were tears of sacrifice, for all the people I loved that I had abandoned for this race."

It was Algeria's first ever gold medal at an Olympic Games and yet she did not get the hero's welcome she had received after the World Championships because the country was still gripped by war and Islamists were critical of her for showing what they perceived as too much of her body.

Instead, Boulmerka returned to see her father, who was in a coma following a stroke. He went on to make a full recovery. She struggled to replicate the heady career heights of 1991 and 1992. Boulmerka won bronze at the 1993 Stuttgart World Championships and a second gold medal at Gothenburg in 1995. It was her last major victory before she retired in 1997.

"IT WAS MY UPBRINGING TO BE REBELLIOUS. YOU TRY TO BE YOUR OWN PERSON, NOT TO FALL INTO A PARTICULAR CATEGORY. YOU HAVE TO DO WHAT YOU FEEL IN YOUR HEART."

Hassiba Boulmerka

Her legacy extends far beyond the records. In pushing back against societal and religious expectations by taking part in sport and by simply wearing shorts, and defying those that delivered death threats or pelted her with rocks while she trained, Boulmerka showed young women in Algeria that they can have options.

The gold in Barcelona "was a triumph for women all over the world to stand up to their enemies," she said. "That's what made me really proud."

As for the way Islamic extremists view the roles of women, Boulmerka explained in the *New York Times*: "A lot of what you hear about the Koran is misinterpreted or blown out of proportion. They do it for political gain.

"It is something natural to run. It was my upbringing to be rebellious. You try to be your own person, not to fall into a particular category. You have to do what you feel in your heart."

BRANDI CHASTAIN

It is one of the most iconic sports images of the twentieth century, one that the *New York Times* described as the "most iconic photograph ever taken of a female athlete." After scoring the winning penalty in the 1999 FIFA Women's World Cup final against China, Brandi Chastain whipped off her shirt – exposing her black sports bra – waved it over her head, and slid onto her knees, head back, eyes closed, fists clenched.

This image is still there for all to see, cast in bronze, outside the Rose Bowl in Pasadena, California. It was there, 20 years earlier, that 90,185 fans had witnessed the drama in person.

"I don't think there's enough words to explain that moment," Chastain told *USA Today* in 2019. "Everyone will look at that differently."

On July 10, 1999, US goalkeeper Briana Scurry saved the penalty attempt from China's Liu Ying and so Chastain walked to the spot with the game in her hands. She was taking the fifth penalty, but that had not been the plan. Having hit the crossbar from the spot in a friendly with China three months prior to the World Cup final, she was bumped down the list by assistant coach Lauren Gregg. However, manager Tony DiCicco had shifted her back up the pecking order, but also suggested the two-footed player hit the ball with her left foot as her right-footed penalties had become too predictable.

"It got to the point that goalkeepers knew where she would kick," DiCicco said in *Twelve Yards: The Art and Psychology of the Perfect Penalty*.

"I didn't think anything of it at the time," Chastain said in the same piece. "I was always ambidextrous and so it always felt normal to use both feet. When I injured my right ankle, I used my left foot to drive the ball a lot more."

Chastain was everything Mia Hamm, the team's reluctant star, was not. She was nicknamed "Hollywood" by her teammates because she loved the pressure of the spotlight. "Brandi wants to have the responsibility on her," said DiCicco. "Some players are afraid of failure, they don't want the role. Brandi wants it. She wants the spotlight. That's the type of player you want in penalty kicks."

There was no greater pressure than that moment in 1999. Beyond the hopes of the team and the crowd, Chastain, who had scored an own goal in the quarter-final against Germany then scored the equalizer, was carrying the growth potential of women's football on her shoulders too.

"It was complete slow-motion between my foot and the net. I've been in a car accident before, not a serious one, and just before it happened, everything went slow but there's nothing you could do to change it," she said of that moment 12 yards out. "It seemed to take forever and while it travelled, everything was so quiet and still and slow. And when it hit the net: an explosion! Noise, cheering, cameras, teammates, everything."

The celebration was far from premeditated. Chastain had shifted from striker to full-back to win a place in the squad at the World Cup, having been dropped for the 1995 edition of the tournament.

"Come on, I'm a left-back in a World Cup final, I'm hardly thinking this game will be my moment. It was a combination of things: joy, relief,

"WHEN IT HIT THE NET: AN EXPLOSION! NOISE, CHEERING, CAMERAS, TEAMMATES, EVERYTHING."

Brandi Chastain

satisfaction, the desire to do well for your team, your country, your family – those are emotions that you carry around every day for years and finally I could let it all out. Put all those things together and what you get is insanity."

"The bra heard 'round the world" read some headlines – a play on the "shot heard round the world" used after Bobby Thomson's home run in 1951 (a famous moment in baseball). The impact of that moment was – and is – immeasurable. It challenged the perception of what a female athlete should look like, strong, athletic, the scars from her knee surgeries visible. It showed that, just like the men, women can get lost in a moment of pure spontaneous joy too. It highlighted the huge dearth of sportswear for women and was a symbol of the struggle for equality.

"You'll make history. And headlines," she said in "A letter to my younger self" for the *Players' Tribune*.

"You can't prepare for the media onslaught that will befall you but embrace it. Don't listen to the sexist remarks about removing your shirt. When you do interview after interview, where everyone asks why, be yourself. Own it. That image will become one of the most iconic in all of sports history. It will stand for glory. For so long, female soccer players lived in an anonymous world with the desperate desire for the sport to be mainstream. Women wanted young girls to have something to aspire to — to see it. So do every interview you have to. Drive the conversation. Give soccer a voice. You've already given it an image."

BÉATRICE HESS

At the 2000 Sydney Olympic Games, Australian swimmer Ian Thorpe, nicknamed "The Thorpedo", ruled the pool, winning three gold and two silver medals.

A few weeks after the Olympic Games, however, a lesser-known swimmer, Béatrice Hess, would earn the nickname "The French Thorpedo" at the 2000 Paralympic Games, winning seven gold medals and breaking a staggering nine world records.

The comparison to Thorpe is one she welcomed, keen to be known as the best ever. "I want to be remembered in Paralympic history – you have Ian Thorpe, why not Béatrice Hess?" she asked.

Hess was no stranger to the Paralympics. At 38 years old, the Frenchwoman had already collected 11 gold medals across three Games, competing in the 1984 International Games for the Disabled (essentially the Paralympics) in New York, the 1988 Seoul Paralympics and 1996 Atlanta Paralympics, but it was at the 2000 Games where she made her biggest splash. She went on to win two more golds at the Athens 2004 Paralympics.

> ## "I WANT TO BE REMEMBERED IN PARALYMPIC HISTORY - YOU HAVE IAN THORPE, WHY NOT BÉATRICE HESS?"
>
> **Béatrice Hess**

Born with cerebral palsy, Hess had been in a wheelchair since the age of 12 and competed in the S5 disability classification. She credited her disability with keeping her away from life sat at a desk.

"I have the chance to live a life unlike everyone else, an unusual life, an almost special life that I would never have lived if I had been able-bodied; that is sure and certain," she told l'Humanité in 2000. "Without my wheelchair and without swimming, I would have been a paper pusher. Look, one of my sisters has spent her life cutting fabric all day long, all week long, all through the last few years. I know that she is always impatient for me to come home so that I can tell her everything I have seen and experienced. Today, I can say that I am lucky to be in a wheelchair."

At the Atlanta Paralympic Games, Hess won six golds and was motivated by a desire to prove the impossible was possible. "I wanted to do what I did in Atlanta because everybody says it's impossible; I want to show it's possible if you work hard," she said.

"I give the medals to my children and my brother-in-law, who has cancer. You need someone else to think about and to motivate you.

"I was scared that I wouldn't do it, because the standard is so high."

"YOU NEED SOMEONE ELSE TO THINK ABOUT AND TO MOTIVATE YOU."

Béatrice Hess

By the Sydney Paralympics, the desire to push beyond the sixth gold medal wasn't strong, but she did, breaking nine world records before her final her nominations for the race. Those efforts earned her nomination for the Laureus World Sportsperson of the Year With A Disability Award in 2000 – and she was nominated again in 2001. Two of those world records from 2000 still stand, in the 200m S5 freestyle and the 20 points 4 x 50m medley relay.

Despite her heroics in the pool, Hess is not a household name. She does not have the profile of Paralympic swimmers such as Americans Trischa Zorn or Jessica Long, or Team GB's Ellie Simmonds. Yet only Zorn (12 in Seoul 1988) and Australia's Jacqueline Freney (eight in London 2012) have won more Paralympic golds in a single Games, and only Japan's Mayumi Narita, Netherlands swimmer Marijke Ruiter and the US's Elizabeth Scott and Erin Popovich have matched her tally of seven gold medals at a single Paralympic Games.

In the small French town of of Étueffont, near the borders of Switzerland and Germany, there is one tribute to Hess, a small swimming pool which bears her name.

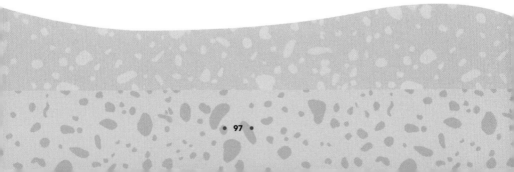

CATHY FREEMAN

When Cathy Freeman won gold medals in the 200m and 400m at the Commonwealth Games at Victoria in Canada in 1994, she completed her victory lap draped in the Australian flag and the black, yellow and red flag of the Indigenous population.

It was a breakout year for Freeman, who had been the first ever Australian Indigenous athlete – her mother of Kuku Yalanji heritage and her father of the Birri Gubba people – to win a gold medal at the Commonweath Games in the 4x100m at Auckland in 1990.

She won silver in the 400m at the Atlanta Olympics in 1996, gold in the 400m at the 1997 Athens World Championships and, with a home Olympics on the horizon, she won another 400m at the 1999 Seville World Championships.

Going into the 2000 Sydney Olympic Games the expectation was huge. Freeman was selected to light the Olympic flame at a spectacular Opening Ceremony in front of 112,000 spectators in the Olympic Stadium, but this was just the curtain-raiser. The pressure came from inside as much as it did from outside. Freeman, who was a talented athlete from an early age, had told a teacher, when she was 14, that

"MY ANCESTORS WERE THE FIRST PEOPLE TO WALK ON THIS LAND. IT'S A REALLY POWERFUL FORCE."

Cathy Freeman

her only career goal was to win an Olympic medal. She had a silver but now, that dream was on the verge of taking her one step further.

Freeman was expected to battle rival and defending 400m Olympic champion Marie-José Pérec for the gold medal, but the Frenchwoman withdrew just before the first round, and fled to Singapore and then Paris, citing threats and insults as the reason for her withdrawal.

With the way cleared somewhat by Pérec's absence, Freeman, wearing her iconic green, white and gold full-body suit with its hood up and red, black and yellow shoes, raced into the history books in a time of 49.11 seconds. She became only the second Australian Indigenous Olympic champion – Nova Peris-Kneebone won gold in the 1996 Atlanta women's hockey tournament and, having switched sports, also competed in the 2000 Olympics 400m.

Once more she held the two flags aloft on her victory lap, despite unofficial flags being banned at the Games.

The significance of Freeman's win cannot be overstated. Just a few months prior, on May 28, more than 250,000 Australians had marched through Sydney in support of reconciliation between Australia's Indigenous and non-Indigenous peoples.

Freeman's Olympic gold was a part of that movement, uniting the country and giving a glimpse of what a reconciliation could look like.

For Freeman, who said in a documentary about her that she was "quite embarrassed to be a Black kid" when young, it was also the culmination of her personal journey.

"An Indigenous kid sort of grew up with that self-image. I could

"I KNOW HOW TO DO THIS. I CAN DO THIS IN MY SLEEP. I CAN WIN THIS. WILL WIN THIS. WHO CAN STOP ME?"

Cathy Freeman

never understand why, whenever I smiled at someone, they wouldn't smile back. I used to get really upset. I thought, why don't people smile back at me? Quietly, it really devastated me."

Freeman sensed she was "being protected", and described her feelings leading up to the race: "My ancestors were the first people to walk on this land. It's a really powerful force. Those other girls were always going to have to come up against my ancestors. For the first time, I feel the stadium, I feel the people, I feel the energy. I feel like I'm being carried. I know exactly what I need to do. I know how to do this. I can do this in my sleep. I can win this. Will win this. Who can stop me?"

Since retiring, Freeman has been at the forefront of the battle for reconciliation and rights for the Indigenous population and her foundation runs educational programmes for 1,600 Indigenous communities across the remote Palm Island, Woorabinda, Wurrumiyanga and Galiwin'ku.

SERENA WILLIAMS

If Althea Gibson opened doors for African-American tennis players, then Venus and Serena Williams have burst through it, held it open and dominated to such an extent that, with the world watching, it was impossible for young African-American women – Sloane Stephens, Madison Keyes, Taylor Townsend, Coco Gauff and more – not to take inspiration from them.

Accessibility and opportunities in tennis for women, ethnic minorities and the working classes are still limited, but now there is a steady conveyor belt of young African-American women tennis players following the path trod by the sisters directly citing them as their motivation for success.

The beginning of the Williams' sisters' story is one of chance. Compton (a troubled Los Angeles suburb) man and cotton-picker's son Richard Williams were channel-surfing but paused on the images of Romanian tennis player Virginia Ruzici being presented with a $40,000 cheque after winning a tennis tournament. At that moment he decided tennis would be the future of his next children.

Venus and Serena, separated by 15 months, were home-schooled by their father and the latter started playing tennis aged four. When Serena was nine and Venus 10, the family moved to West Palm Beach in Florida so they could attend Rick Macci's tennis academy. Macci was impressed watching them practise, but was properly taken by the pair when they played competitively for points.

"I could see the speed, the quickness, and I knew how tall they were going to be," he told the *Guardian*. "I went right up to Richard and I said, 'Let me tell you something. You've got the next female Michael Jordan on your hands.' He puts his arm around me and he goes, 'No, brother man, I got the next two.'"

It was eerily prophetic for the man with zero tennis coaching experience before he embarked on his tennis takeover project. Now, the pair have a staggering 122 career singles titles between them.

Serena's statistics are especially staggering. She has won 23 Grand Slam singles championships, one fewer than the record-holding Australian Margaret Court, and 39 Grand Slam titles when her doubles and mixed doubles titles are included. Her other achievements include:

- The only American player, male or female, to win more than 20 Grand Slam singles championships.
- Holds the record for the most women's singles matches won at Grand Slams with 365.
- The most recent holder of all four women's Grand Slam singles titles simultaneously, and only the third player to achieve it twice (in 2002–03 and 2014–15).
- The most recent winner of women's major titles on clay, grass and hard courts in the same calendar year, known as the Surface Slam.
- The winner of a record 13 women's Grand Slams on hard courts.
- Holds the women's Open Era record for most singles titles at the Australian Open with seven wins and her six US Open championships are matched only by Chris Evert.
- Serena and Venus are the only tennis players to win four Olympic gold medals (one singles each and three doubles together).

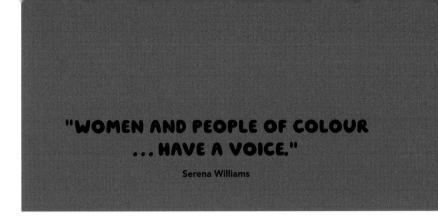

"WOMEN AND PEOPLE OF COLOUR ... HAVE A VOICE."

Serena Williams

In many respects Venus' and Serena's off-court activities have helped them transcend tennis and sport generally. Both campaigned for equal prize money at Wimbledon and the French Open, continuing the fight of Billie Jean King and her peers. Both have spent their careers fighting racism and misogyny, with Serena boycotting the BNP Paribas Open tournament at the Indian Wells, California, resort for 14 years after being subjected to racist abuse there.

Serena has repeatedly called out the double standards in officiating and in the media when she has reacted angrily on the court, comparing her situation to those of men's players who have been similarly outspoken. When returning to action following the birth of her daughter, her black catsuit, designed to help her circulation after a history of blood clots and a pulmonary embolism after giving birth left her bedridden, was banned from future tournaments. The French Tennis Federation president, Bernard Giudicelli, said: "I believe we have sometimes gone too far. Serena's outfit this year, for example, would no longer be accepted. You have to respect the game and the place."

The grind is relentless, but Serena has embraced it. Never shying away from confronting those attempting to undermine her success or incidents of discrimination based on her race or sex.

"Maybe it doesn't get better in time for me," she told *Vogue*. "But someone in my position can show women and people of colour that we have a voice, because Lord knows I use mine."

WOJDAN SHAHERKANI

Wojdan Shaherkani's Olympic Games career was fleeting, but the impact of those 82 seconds was immeasurable. Shaherkani's journey to the judo mat at the ExCeL Centre in east London in 2012 was fraught, but the 16-year-old strode away from her brief match with Puerto Rico's Melissa Mojica at half-heavyweight, 78kg, to a standing ovation.

Shaherkani was born in Messner in Saudi Arabia, a country where women's rights are severely restricted. Her father, Ali Shaherkani, was a judo referee and his daughter began to take it up. In early 2012 she earned her blue belt and, months later, she was in London.

The International Olympic Committee has a long-standing policy for all countries participating in the Games to have both women and men competing. In June 2012, the ban on female Olympians was lifted in Saudi Arabia, but harsh restrictions on women's and girls' involvement in sport still existed and the standard of Saudi women competitors was far below the international standards required for them to qualify.

The closest any female athlete from Saudi Arabia got to traditional qualification was showjumper Dalma Rushdi Malhas, who won a bronze medal at the 2010 Youth Olympics, but even she fell short of qualifying for London 2012.

The three countries that had never previously sent a female athlete to the Olympics, Saudi Arabia, Brunei and Qatar, were given special wild card clearance by the IOC for their women athletes to compete and so Saudis Shaherkani and 800m runner Sarah Attar were cleared to participate at London 2012.

"This is very positive news and we will be delighted to welcome these two athletes in London in a few weeks' time," IOC President Jacques Rogge said in a statement at the time.

"The IOC has been working very closely with the Saudi Arabian Olympic Committee and I am pleased to see that our continued dialogue has come to fruition. The IOC has been striving to ensure a greater gender balance at the Olympic Games, and today's news can be seen as an encouraging evolution."

The backlash at home was brutal. The perception was that the country had yielded to international pressure in fear of possible sanctions. The Saudi Arabia Olympic Committee decided not to promote their young athletes' participation in the London Games and stipulated that their two women competitors could only take part if they wore a hijab, dressed modestly, did not mix with men and were accompanied by a male guardian at all times.

On the eve of the Games there was further controversy when the International Judo Federation announced that Shaherkani would not be permitted to wear a hijab while competing. Their main, flawed, argument was that it was a safety hazard, despite the Judo Union of Asia allowing the hijab to be worn in their competitions. "In Judo, we use strangleholds and chokeholds so the hijab could be dangerous," IJF spokesman Nicolas Messner said.

Eventually the IJF and IOC reached an agreement over the 16-year-old wearing a modified hijab, akin to a swimming cap.

It was against this backdrop of controversy, pressures and abuse that Shaherkani took to the mat.

"In white," the announcer declared, "the first woman ever from Saudi Arabia, Wojdan Shaherkani."

Her 82-second loss was the second shortest match in that weight class, with Japan's Mika Sugimoto beating Brazilian Maria Suelen Altheman in 48 seconds.

"I WAS SCARED A LOT, BECAUSE OF ALL THE CROWD AROUND ... I'M EXCITED AND PROUD TO BE REPRESENTING MY COUNTRY."

Wojdan Shaherkani

"I was scared a lot, because of all the crowd around and lost, because this is the first time," Shaherkani said afterwards. "I'm excited and proud to be representing my country. Unfortunately, I lost but hopefully I'll do better next time … Hopefully this will be the start of bigger participation for other sports also … Hopefully this is the beginning of a new era."

Her father said he "cried like a baby" watching his daughter finally compete. "She was happy and smiled when she finished the fight," he said. "She hugged me and said: 'Daddy, I did this.' I was so proud."

Shaherkani and Attar forced the door open for Saudi Arabian women to be able to compete at Olympic Games, but sport is still incredibly inaccessible for women in Saudi Arabia. At Rio 2016, Attar was joined by three other women, Kariman Abuljadayel, Lubna Al-Omair and Joud Fahmy, in an 11-strong Saudi Arabian delegation to the Games. And, at the Covid-delayed 2020 Tokyo Games there were two female competitors, sprinter Yasmeen Al-Dabbagh – who was the Saudi flag-bearer at the Opening Ceremony – and judo's Tahani Alqahtani.

NICOLA ADAMS

Women's boxing has a rich history and can be traced as far back as the early eighteenth century when bare-knuckle boxer Elizabeth Wilkinson from Clerkenwell in London is believed to have competed. The first women's boxing club was founded in the 1920s in London. From the outset, though, women boxers have had to struggle against sexist attitudes and social norms for the right to compete.

The sport's inclusion in the Olympic Games was a long road. Men's boxing was introduced into the third Olympics, at the 1904 Games in St Louis, and became a fixture of the four-yearly event. Women also featured that year in an exhibition contest, but it would not be made a permanent feature.

Instead, they had to wait 105 years before the International Olympic Committee's Executive Board approved the inclusion of women's boxing at future Games. Three years later, on Sunday, August 5, 2012, the first two of eight women flyweights entered the ring at the ExCeL Exhibition Centre in the round of 16 at the London Games.

British boxer Natasha Jonas, the sister of England footballer Nikita Parris, was the first ever British female boxer to compete at an Olympic Games But it was Nicola Adams who stole the spotlight, becoming the first female Olympic boxing champion by beating the Chinese world champion Ren Cancan in the flyweight final.

Adams' achievement in 2012 echoed far beyond the ring. Even the most right-wing of news outlets

championed her victory and the explosion of the sport generally. The *Daily Telegraph* said the women's boxing was "the purest distillation of the Olympic spirit – the pursuit of sport for sport's sake," while *The Sun* said, "Emmeline Pankhurst would have been proud" of Jonas.

"Knowing that young girls might be inspired to take up the sport is as good as winning this medal," Adams said after winning her historic gold medal.

"I would love it if there were girls who watched that fight and thought: 'Yes, I can do that.' I got my inspiration when I sat down with my father, at about eight or nine years old, and watched The Rumble in the Jungle. It was amazing watching Muhammad Ali. I watched tapes of Sugar Ray Robinson too – what a terrific left hook.

"I hope, too, that winning here will inspire the rest of the guys and we can get even more gold. I will tell them to relax, keep their focus and they are bound to box at their best. It has been great working with all of them."

Adams' journey to becoming an Olympic champion began when her mother, Denver, took the 12-year-old to the Star and Fitness gym in Leeds just to give the youngster "something to do" while she had an aerobics class. At 13 Adams fought in, and won, her first bout against Claire Newton, from a rival gym. However, the search to find a second opponent took her coaches another four years.

In 2001 she was invited to an England selection training camp and had the opportunity to train alongside the world heavyweight champion, David Haye. She became England's first female boxer that year. Two years later, she was England's first amateur champion and retained that title in the following three championships. Her first major international tournament success came in 2007, when she won silver in the bantamweight (54kg) division at the European Championships at Vejle, Denmark, and she won silver medals at the 2008 and 2010 world championships, the latter after she had taken a spell out with a back injury.

The decision to include women's boxing at the Olympics was a game-changer for the Yorkshire fighter. Adams had worked as a builder and an extra on shows such as *EastEnders*, *Emmerdale* and *Coronation Street* and her mother had worked multiple jobs to help cover the costs of training and competing. However, once women's boxing was made an Olympic sport, official funding became available and money flowed into the sport for the first time.

In the build-up to the 2012 Olympics Adams continued to shine, winning the first GB Amateur Boxing Championship in Liverpool, and then, in 2011, collecting gold at the European Amateur Boxing Championship in Poland.

Having become the first woman to win an Olympic Games boxing gold medal at London 2012, Adams became the inaugural winner of a women's boxing gold at the Glasgow 2014 Commonwealth Games. She then successfully defended her Olympic title at the 2016 Rio Olympics, beating France's Sarah Ourahmoune in the final. After the Games, Adams turned professional and made her debut in April 2017, beating Virginia Carcamo in Manchester. She retired undefeated after two years as the WBO female flyweight world champion.

Away from the ring she has continued to break boundaries. Having come out to her mother when she was 13 and was named the most influential LGBT person in Britain by *The Independent* in 2012 after her Olympic win. Adams clarified that she is a lesbian publicly in 2020, having been frustrated at being referred to as bisexual. She was the first person to be paired in a same-sex couple on *Strictly Come Dancing* in 2021.

She requested a female partner, and explained to the *Guardian*: "I guess it's just breaking those boundaries and showing people that it's OK. It's not such an uncommon thing: professional dancers dance with people of the same sex all the time; you dance in a nightclub with your friends. I just wanted to break down the thing of it being a big deal when it's not really a big deal."

TRISCHA ZORN

There is no competition. Trischa Zorn's 55 Paralympic Games medal haul is more than double the tally of the next most successful athlete, Norway's Ragnhild Myklebust. In her 24-year career Zorn amassed 41 Paralympic gold medals, nine silver and five bronze in backstroke, breaststroke, freestyle, butterfly, individual medley and various relays, across a multitude of distances.

Zorn was born visually impaired, with aniridia blindness, which means she was born without irises to regulate the amount of light absorbed. As a result, she can see rough outlines and shapes of objects up to 20 feet (6 metres) away, but cannot see features and details.

"People ask me how I do it," Zorn told the *Los Angeles Times* in 1986. "They ask if I hit the walls or the lane lines. But it's not really that hard. When I first started swimming, I bumped into the wall a few times, but I usually can see the black line on the bottom of the pool, or on backstroke I look for the flags and count my strokes."

At the age of eight, Zorn caught wind of a swimming team that was being set up locally and she ditched dance and gymnastics to focus on the pool. Two years later, her family moved to Mission Viejo in California, where she swam for the Mission Viejo Nadadores Swim Team from the age of 10 until 18.

"Growing up I did not have a role model per se," she told journalism graduate Jennifer Geminiani.

"My mom always told me to be myself and to always challenge myself by pushing myself to limits that were not expected of a person with a physical disability. I did, however, always align myself with individuals who had the same goals and motivation and who would push me to my limits whether it be in swimming practice, school, or work.

"Getting out of bed early every morning was hard, but I had to be dedicated and disciplined to get to practice and put the work in in order for me to accomplish my goals that I had set for that season or for that particular Paralympic Games."

Her success in the pool in high school prompted a host of scholarship offers and she became the first visually impaired person to receive an athletic scholarship to a Division I college. At the University of Nebraska, Zorn studied special education. She also went on to study school administration and supervision and later law.

Zorn made her Paralympics debut in Arnhem in the Netherlands in 1980 aged 16 and won her first seven gold medals, five in individual events and two in relays. Perhaps most impressively, she was unbeaten in every Paralympic race between 1980 and 1992, across 25 races, winning six golds in 1984 in New York, a staggering 12 gold medals at Seoul 1988, 10 more at Barcelona 1992 and then two more at Atlanta 1996. Her career didn't end there, as she won four silvers at the Sydney Paralympic Games 2000 and, aged 40, a final bronze at the Athens 2004 Paralympics.

Ahead of the Sydney Games in 2000, while she was in law school, Zorn and a number of other Paralympians were invited by Team USA to live and train full-time at the Olympic Training Centre in Colorado Springs. There was huge pressure for her to thrive and continue to blaze a trail, so she took a year out from her studies to take full advantage

> **"MY MOM ALWAYS TOLD ME TO BE MYSELF AND TO ALWAYS CHALLENGE MYSELF BY PUSHING MYSELF TO LIMITS THAT WERE NOT EXPECTED OF A PERSON WITH A PHYSICAL DISABILITY."**
>
> Trischa Zorn

of the opportunity. "I think the expectations were higher than any other Paralympics just because we spent a whole year [in Colorado Springs]," she told the Team USA website. "Really knowing the impact and the consequences this would have on the future, if this were an opportunity or something other athletes would be able to have, I think made it a little more stressful than normal Paralympic Games."

Having retired from international competition, Zorn works for the Department for Veteran Affairs in Indianapolis and, despite her huge medal haul, she counted her biggest win as being inducted into the International Paralympic Hall of Fame.

"Being inducted into the International Paralympic Hall of Fame in 2012 in London was a highlight of my athletic career that no gold medal could be compared to," she said. "I want to believe that I made a positive impact on the sport and on the Paralympic Games.

"I think about it and sometimes wish we were at that point back then, but now I know that the goal of the Paralympic athletes of that generation was to pave the way for the athletes now who have those opportunities."

CHRISTINE SINCLAIR

On September 1, 2021 the headlines were emphatic, Portugal superstar Cristiano Ronaldo had broken the international goal-scoring record with two goals against the Republic of Ireland in FIFA World Cup 2022 qualifying. Very few media outlets added the caveat that his then total of 115 goals in fact sat far behind the 188 scored by Canada Women's National Team forward Christine Sinclair in 306 games.

When Sinclair scored her 184th and 185th goals against St Kitts and Nevis in Concacaf Olympic Games qualifying in January 2020, she surpassed the tally of US World Cup winner and two-time Olympic champion Abby Wambach, who scored 184 in 255 games.

"Thank you to everyone for all the messages. I'm slightly overwhelmed," Sinclair posted on Twitter afterwards. "Thank you to all my teammates, coaches, staff, friends and family, 185 would not have been possible without you."

She told the BBC: "I remember starting my career and thinking, 'I have so many goals to get to', but sort of having my eye on the record as a 16-year-old."

Her career has spanned five World Cups and four Olympics and she was shortlisted for the FIFA World Player of the Year award in 2005,

"I THINK IT'S TIME FOR CANADA TO STEP UP. THAT'S WHAT I HOPE THEY SAW TODAY."

Christine Sinclair

2006, 2007, 2008, 2010, 2012 and 2016. At club level she has won championships with three teams, the 2010 WPS Championship with FC Gold Pride, the 2011 WPS Championship with Western New York Flash and the 2013 and 2017 NWSL Championships with her current team, Portland Thorns.

In 2021, at the Covid-delayed Tokyo 2020 Olympic Games, Sinclair finally tasted victory with the national team, collecting a gold medal as former England assistant manager and now Canada manager, Bev Priestman, masterminded a tactically astute run to the final, where they beat Sweden.

Sinclair's journey started young. Football was in her family: one uncle, Brian Gant, played for the national team and another, Bruce Gant, was close to a call-up for the 1976 Montreal Olympics, while her mother was an under-sevens coach at the local club, where Christine joined aged only four. But soccer wasn't necessarily her sport; she played everything at home – basketball, baseball, volleyball, golf, rollerblading. When she was 11, football took over and, at 15, she was spotted by the then national team manager Even Pellerud, who called her up for the squad, and she made her debut aged 16 in the 2000 Algarve Cup.

She immediately became the focal point of the Canadian attack. "The play was based very much on getting the ball to Christine Sinclair," Pellerud told *SportsNet*. In eight seasons with Pellerud as head coach she scored 95 goals.

In 2001, Sinclair started at the University of Portland, Oregon, USA, in the city that would become her home. In her first season on the university team she scored 23 goals and provided eight assists, leading her to be named *Soccer America's* Freshman of the Year.

"Coming into that program, [head coach] Clive Charles saw me as a young player, but a leader on the team," she told the Portland Thorns website. "He expected a lot from me even as a freshman. I had experienced it before, being young and being in the national team traveling the world. It was such a smooth transition for me and the fact that it was a small school really helped me. I think I would've gotten lost in some of those bigger schools."

In her second season she was Division 1's leading scorer with 26 goals. In the national championship game she scored twice against Santa Clara to give Portland the title. She competed with Canada at the 2003 World Cup in her third year, helping Canada to a best-ever fourth-place finish, then returned to the University of Portland and won the coveted Hermann Trophy – awarded to the best men's and women's college soccer (football) player – after scoring 22 goals. She set the all-time Division 1 goalscoring record in her final year with 39 and won the Hermann Trophy again.

She was the eighth overall pick in the 2008 WPS, America's top professional league, expansion draft that would begin her domestic professional career.

Despite her outstanding efforts on the pitch, Sinclair is a reluctant star who avoids the spotlight as much as is possible. In the final of the Tokyo Olympics, at 38 she was fouled for the penalty which Jessie Fleming converted to equalize. With penalties looming, Priestman replaced Sinclair as legs tired but the record-breaker understood. "We now play to our strengths," she said after Canada won 3–2 on penalties after the game ended 1–1, ensuring Sinclair's international heroics were rewarded with the top prize at a major competition. "Bev definitely brought that to our team and we have a gold medal so she must have done something right."

On becoming Olympic champions, Sinclair called for investment in the future of Canadian football. "I hope we inspired a lot of people back home and I hope we see some investment in the women's game," she said. "I think it's time Canada gets a professional league or some professional teams and if a gold medal and three Olympic medals doesn't do that, nothing will. I think it's time for Canada to step up. That's what I hope they saw today."

RACHAEL BLACKMORE

"I don't feel male or female right now. I don't even feel human,"
elated jockey Rachael Blackmore said after her historic Grand
National win on Minella Times. The iconic statement came after
she had become the first woman jockey to ride the winner of
the world's most famous jumps race.

Prior to Blackmore's victory in April 2021, 32 female riders had attempted to break one of horseracing's highest glass ceilings. Only one had finished in the first four, Katie Walsh on Seabass in 2012.

"I'm delighted for Rachael," said Walsh. "This isn't just pot luck or a fluke, she's worked hard to get this.

"She's an inspiration to male and female jockeys. This is the most-watched race in the world and it's just brilliant for horse racing."

The only cloud over Blackmore's Grand National win was the lack of a 100,000-strong crowd that usually files into Aintree for the showpiece race of the year, with Covid restrictions denying the jockey the roar of the crowd.

"I just got such an unbelievable passage through the race," Blackmore said afterwards. "Minella Times just jumped fantastic and brought me from fence to fence. Ruby Walsh and Katie Walsh, I've asked them both in the past about riding around here and they often talk about a semi-circle in front of you and I felt like I had that everywhere.

"That is what you need in a race like this, you need so much luck to get around with no one else interfering first of all. You need so much to go right, and things went right for me today. I feel

so incredibly lucky. It is unbelievable, I'm just so thrilled.

"What Henry de Bromhead [Minella Times's trainer] does with these horses, I don't know! I'm so lucky to be riding them, I just cannot believe I'm after winning the Grand National. This is unbelievable."

De Bromhead said of his rider: "She's tough and brilliant. You can see that [after] she joined us, we have gone from strength to strength with her. She's a fantastic rider, a great team player and just a lovely person to work with. She's breaking through all the records."

Blackmore grew up around horses. The daughter of a dairy farmer and a schoolteacher, she grew up on her parents' farm in Tipperary. She was given her first horse, named Bubbles, aged seven and she began taking part in pony racing competitions, pony club meetings and hunting and, by 13, she had been well and truly "bitten by the racing bug".

One inspiration was the film *National Velvet* starring Elizabeth Taylor. "*National Velvet* was definitely something that would have been on the television when we were growing up," she said to the BBC in April 2021 of the 1944 film in which Taylor plays 12-year-old Velvet Brown, who won the Grand National before being disqualified on a technicality.

"We knew she was competitive – Charles [her father] taught her how to ride and negotiate obstacles, and at a very young age she wanted to jump everything Jonathan [her brother] jumped," said her mother, Eimir.

Blackmore studied equine science in Limerick and told the *Irish Times* in 2019 that she had never envisaged a career in racing. "I always wanted to be an amateur jockey and ride in races, but I never envisaged the professional jockey route. It was not a career I thought would work out for me," she said.

"I grew up on a farm and always had ponies and did a lot of pony clubs, hunts and races, and had my first win at 13 at a pony race in Cork, beating Paul Townend [now a fellow top professional jockey]."

"I JUST HOPE IT SHOWS IT DOESN'T MATTER, MALE OR FEMALE."

Rachael Blackmore

Her first amateur win came in 2011 on Stowaway Pearl and, four years later, she became the first Irish woman to turn professional since Maria Cullen in the 1980s. In 2017 she became the first woman to win the Irish Conditional Riders Championship.

In terms of quality and quantity, the Cheltenham Festival is the world's best jumps horse racing meeting and in 2021, Blackmore rode six winners, a total only ever beaten by Ruby Walsh, who twice won seven. At the 2022 Cheltenham Festival she repeated her Champion Hurdle victory on Honeysuckle and then became the first female jockey to triumph in the Cheltenham Gold Cup, riding A Plus Tard, winning by 15 lengths.

After her Grand National win, Blackmore shrugged off her history-making antics. "Ah, look, it's brilliant, but I won't be the last. I'm delighted for myself anyway," she said. "I just hope it shows it doesn't matter, male or female. Plenty of people have gone before me and done that – Katie Walsh was third here on Seabass. All those things help girls coming along, but I don't think it's a major talking point any more."

ELISABETA LIPĂ

Elisabeta Lipă took up rowing at 16 and immediately impressed, winning a bronze medal in the women's coxed quadruple sculls at the 1981 World Rowing Junior Championships at Sofia, Bulgaria. Her continued good success earned selection for the Romanian team at the 1984 Los Angeles Olympic Games and she won her first Olympic gold medal in the double sculls event.

The medals kept coming. Her gold in Los Angeles kickstarted an Olympic gold run, winning in the single sculls at Barcelona 1992, and as part of eight at Atlanta 1996, Sydney 2000 and Athens 2004. She also won two double sculls silver medals at Seoul 1988 and Barcelona (both times partnering Veronica Cochela) and a bronze in the quadruple sculls at Seoul.

"I wish I was 20 years younger, or maybe even more, so I could relive the World Championships and the Olympic Games," she told World Rowing.com in 2019.

She was awarded the Thomas Keller Medal, the World Rowing Federation's award for an outstanding international rowing career in 2008 and was named the Best Rower of the

"I WISH I WAS 20 YEARS YOUNGER, OR MAYBE EVEN MORE, SO I COULD RELIVE THE WORLD CHAMPION- SHIPS AND THE OLYMPIC GAMES."

Elisabeta Lipă

20th Century by the International Rowing Federation.

Now, her ability to exercise is limited.

"I try to stay in shape by doing the exercises recommended by my doctor, so I guess you could say that I'm still active," she said.

Despite her retirement after the Athens 2004 Olympics, having become the oldest oarswoman – two months short of her 40th birthday – to win an Olympic gold and the first rower to win eight Olympic medals, Lipă is still very involved in the sport. Between 2015 and 2017 she was the minister for youth and sport in Romania and she has also been president of the Romanian Rowing Federation, but her family has borne the brunt of her efforts to progress the sport.

"My family accepted my career decision. My sacrifices were also their sacrifices. They have always supported me throughout my career. They are, and have always been, extremely proud of me," she said.

Now, she is moulding the next generation. "I want them to work

"I FEEL AS THOUGH IT IS MY RESPONSIBILITY TO PASS ON ALL OF MY KNOWLEDGE IN ORDER TO SHAPE THE NEW GENERATION OF ROWING ATHLETES."

Elisabeta Lipă

hard, to be dedicated, to make sacrifices, because life as a professional athlete is quite beautiful. I remind them of this each and every day, at every occasion, be it when we're training or right before a competition," she said.

"I've always been grateful to the country and the sport that granted me my notoriety and my reputation, and so I feel as though it is my responsibility to pass on all of my knowledge in order to shape the new generation of rowing athletes."

AMÉLIE MAURESMO

In spring 2014, defending Wimbledon champion Andy Murray told Sky Sports that as rumours he might be about to begin working with a female coach circulated, he started getting messages from other players and from their coaches. "'I can't believe you're playing this game with the media. You should tell them tomorrow you're considering working with a dog'," he relayed.

The questioning did not just come from those on the tour with him. The 1977 Wimbledon champion Virginia Wade reportedly called the hire "a joke" and said that Murray was trying to "mess people around" by appointing a woman.

The pressure, then, when former Wimbledon and Australian Open champion-turned-coach Amélie Mauresmo agreed to take on the high-profile Murray, was huge.

"When Andy Murray first came to pick me up, I thought it was bullshit, it was a hoax," she told Eurosport.

"It had never been done in men's tennis, or at least it hadn't been done very much.

"I had the impression that I had a lot of responsibility and that I didn't have the right to make mistakes. If I screwed up, all women would screw up with me."

Mauresmo was not totally new to coaching men. She began her coaching career with Michaël Llodra in 2010, before swapping to women players, coaching Victoria Azarenka in 2012 and Marion Bartoli in 2013, but Murray's profile and rank was another level. She teamed up with Murray, whose recent triumphs had included two Grand

Slams, including a historic first Wimbledon win, and the London 2012 Olympic Games gold medal.

In many respects, female tennis coaches owe as much to Murray's mother Judy as they do to Mauresmo and Murray for breaking the mould. Judy, who played tennis and badminton before turning to coaching, experienced the inequalities in tennis from bottom to top herself and was forced to battle sexist stereotypes as the mother and former coach of Britain's number one. She had been labelled a "pushy parent" until, she says, she was "forgiven" by tennis fans when Murray won Wimbledon, and was recently recognized for her pioneering role in the development of grassroots tennis and the rise of Murray and his brother Jamie. Growing up in the presence of a female coach and in an environment where women's tennis was respected will have undoubtedly helped shape Murray's views.

"I knew it hadn't happened before, but I wasn't thinking of it being a ground-breaking move or having an influence that could cross over into other sports," he said of the reaction to appointing Mauresmo. "After seeing the response to it, and some of the things that have been said, I can see it is. I've actually become very passionate about getting more women in sport, giving women more opportunities. When I was younger, I wasn't thinking about stuff like that. But now I've seen it with my own eyes, it's quite amazing how few female coaches there are across any sport."

The scrutiny was intense. Coaches are judged on the performances of their players, but often they are given the benefit of time and are reviewed based on a collection of performances. From the off, each of Murray's matches, win or lose, saw Mauresmo's coaching credentials analyzed and questioned.

Mauresmo's two years with Murray did not yield a Grand Slam title, but there were caveats. Yes, Murray had had a hugely successful year prior, but back surgery in September 2013 meant he was out for three months and didn't train at 100 per cent until August 2014. The

French coach helped him recover from that time out and move back up the rankings, into the top five and rising as high as number two in the world. During their time working together, Murray's record on clay courts improved and he won his first tour-level clay court titles in Madrid and Munich. He also reached the final of the Australian Open. After the two-year partnership ended in May 2016, Murray went on to have perhaps his best season, winning a second Wimbledon, retaining his Olympic gold medal, claiming nine ATP tournaments, reaching three Grand Slam finals, spending 41 weeks at number one and ending the year with a 24-match winning streak.

Mauresmo took over as coach of Frenchman Lucas Pouille for the 2019 season and helped him reach the Australian Open semi-final – losing to Novak Djokovic – having never previously won a match in the tournament.

Mauresmo's work with Murray was game-changing. It started conversations not only about a lack of opportunities for female coaches, but also – with the Frenchwoman having had her first child during her time with Murray – on parenthood in sport and brought working mothers generally into the spotlight. When Martina Navratilova was included in conversations about becoming Murray's coach without much furore it was clear how much impact Mauresmo had made. In addition, more women now coach in women's tennis.

Following the landmark decision, Agnieszka Radwanska hired Navratilova and Madison Keys hired Lindsay Davenport, with the latter telling ESPN: "You have to credit Murray for taking that plunge. Andy has been phenomenal with his support, and he was raised by a strong mother … I hope that in a few years we will look back and think: 'Why was this such a big deal?' It seems that we go like that with social issues around the world and giving everyone equal rights, and maybe the same thing will happen with women coaching men."

Navratilova told the *Independent*: "Amélie opened the door and maybe other players won't care one way or the other about the gender."

KIRAN GANDHI

Kiran Gandhi has never been a professional athlete, she is a music producer and activist who was a drummer for M.I.A. However, in 2015, her decision to run the London Marathon for Breast Cancer Care was more impactful than she could perhaps have ever imagined. Gandhi had not planned to make a statement but, the night before the marathon she had trained a year for, her period started.

In her 12 months of preparation, she had not run on the first or second days of her period due to the intense pain. But she had raised more than £4,800 for charity.

"I went through my options. Running 26.2 miles with a wad of cotton material wedged between my legs just seemed so absurd," she wrote in the *Absurdist*. "Plus, they say chafing can be a real problem. I honestly didn't know what to do. I knew that I was lucky to have access to sanitary products, and to be part of a society that at least treats periods with a degree of normality. I could definitely choose to participate in this norm at the expense of my own comfort and just deal with it quietly. But then I thought … If there's one person society can't eff with, it's a marathon runner. You can't tell a

"RUNNING 26.2 MILES WITH A WAD OF COTTON MATERIAL WEDGED BETWEEN MY LEGS SEEMED SO ABSURD."

Kiran Gandhi

marathoner to clean themselves up, or to prioritize the comfort of others over theirs. On the marathon course, I could choose whether or not I wanted to participate in this status quo of shaming. I decided to just take some Midol, hope I wouldn't cramp, bleed freely and just run."

So that is what she did. As she ran, she let the blood flow with the intention of highlighting the crazy scenario half the population is forced to keep quiet about or be ashamed about every month.

"As I ran, I thought to myself about how women and men have been socialized to pretend periods don't exist," she says in her mile-by-mile account. "Through period-shaming, society prevents us from bonding over an experience that 50 per cent of the world's population share monthly.

"By making it difficult to speak about, we don't have language to express period pain in the workplace. Such differences between women and men should be accepted, but they're not. Because it's all kept quiet, women are made to think that they shouldn't complain or talk about their own bodily functions, since no-one can see it happening. And if you can't see it, it's probably 'not a big deal'. Why is this an important issue? Because 'this' is happening, right now, everywhere."

She crossed the finish line in 4:49:11 flanked by close friends Ana and Mere who, despite having run marathons before, stuck by Gandhi's side the whole way.

En route, she was buoyed by the cheering of her father and brother,

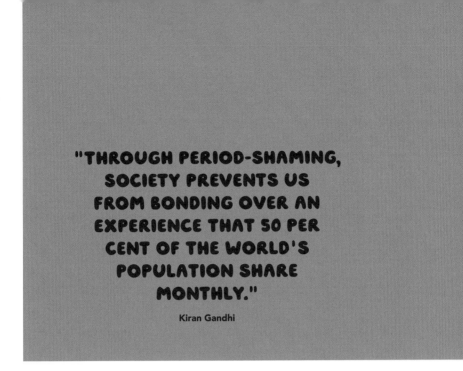

"THROUGH PERIOD-SHAMING, SOCIETY PREVENTS US FROM BONDING OVER AN EXPERIENCE THAT 50 PER CENT OF THE WORLD'S POPULATION SHARE MONTHLY."

Kiran Gandhi

who were absorbed by the moment and did not care about the red between her legs.

The impact was huge. The images of Gandhi's blood-stained leggings were everywhere. Good and bad, comments sections on articles and chat shows were discussing periods, period poverty, hygiene, and more. Women felt empowered and emboldened by her actions and were discussing their own period woes. The tool for her unplanned protest, the London Marathon, made sense. For decades marathons have been used by people to push themselves to the limits and to highlight causes. It wasn't until Kathrine Switzer gate-crashed the Boston Marathon 48 years earlier that women had even been allowed to run. In 2015 Gandhi's action was the latest in a long line of breakthrough moments for women in an iconic test of endurance.

CASTER SEMENYA

"I am Mokgadi Caster Semenya. I am a woman and I am fast."

At the African Junior Championships at the end of July 2009, when she was 18 years old, Caster Semenya ran the 800m in 1:56.72. In doing so she beat her personal best, set nine months earlier, by seven seconds, and recorded the fasted time of 2009 until that point. The following month, she won her first 800m World Championship gold medal in a time of 1:55.45, two and a half seconds ahead of her nearest rival. Except, instead of celebrating her athletic prowess, in the same way Michael Phelps' flipper-like feet or Usain Bolt's abnormally large legs and stride have attracted global acclaim and legions of fans, Semenya found her gender questioned to the extent that the IAAF demanded she took a gender verification test.

The announcement was controversial in and of itself because it allowed suspicion to reign and engulf the 18-year-old from Limpopo, whereas the press is only notified of doping tests if both A and B samples have tested positive. Instead, everything from Semenya's physique to her voice and her choice of clothes was scrutinized while the world waited to find out the results of her gender test. The IAAF was accused of racism and sexism.

"Since my victory in the female 800-metre event at the Berlin World Championships in August last year, I have been subjected to unwarranted and invasive scrutiny of the most intimate and private details of my being," she said in a statement

announcing her return to competition while the findings were still pending. "Some of the occurrences leading up to and immediately following the Berlin World Championships have infringed on not only my rights as an athlete but also my fundamental and human rights, including my rights to dignity and privacy."

The findings were never made public, but Semenya was cleared to run by the IAAF in 2010 and won 800m gold medals at the London 2012 and Rio 2016 Olympic Games, the Daegu 2011 and London 2017 World Championships, Asaba 2016 and Durban 2018 African Championships, plus further gold medals in the 400m (Asaba), 1,500m and 4 x 400m relay (Durban). The London Olympics gold was upgraded from silver after Russian athlete Mariya Savinova was retrospectively disqualified after being found guilty after failing a drugs test.

Semenya was not completely free to run, however. Between 2010 and 2015, she was forced to take testosterone-supressing medication which she has since said affected her mental and physical health.

After her victory in Rio in 2016, British runner Lynsey Sharp, who finished sixth, slammed her participation while fifth-placed Joana Jóźwik, from Poland, went further when she said: "I feel like the silver medallist … I'm glad I'm the first European, the second white [to finish the race]." It was a horrifically racist comment.

In 2018 the IAAF unveiled new rules which required athletes who have certain disorders of sex development that cause testosterone levels over 5 nmol/L (nanomoles per litre) to medically lower their testosterone to compete in eight female events, including the 400m, 800m and 1500m events commonly contested by Semenya. She legally challenged the rules.

"The IAAF used me in the past as a human guinea pig to experiment with how the medication they required me to take would affect my testosterone levels," she said. "Even though the hormonal drugs made me feel constantly sick, the IAAF now wants to enforce even stricter thresholds with unknown health consequences.

"I will not allow the IAAF to use me and my body again. But I am concerned that other female athletes will feel compelled to let the IAAF drug them and test the effectiveness and negative health effects of different hormonal drugs. This cannot be allowed to happen."

The challenge was rejected and Semenya appealed to the Federal Supreme Court of Switzerland but it was also rejected.

Semenya has refused to take medication to supress her testosterone levels again. She instead decided to switch to shorter distances not covered by the 400m to one mile ban, but decided against competing at the Tokyo Olympics in 2021.

Her determination to defend her right to run as a woman, unhindered by drugs, has been truly incredible in the face of the most brutal of examinations and scrutiny from a very young age.

"It's taking the soul out of my body," she told the *Guardian* in 2021. "They want me to take my own system down. I'm not sick. I don't need drugs. I will never do that.

"I trained like a slave to be the greatest," she said. "I've watched Usain Bolt train. His training was insane and I am the same. My high testosterone levels are something I was born with, it's a disorder. It doesn't make me the best, though. That's where the training and knowledge comes in.

"Michael Phelps's arms are wide enough for him to do whatever he wants. Swimmers' lungs are different to other people's. Basketball players like LeBron James are tall. If all the tall players are banned from playing, will basketball be the same? Usain has amazing muscle fibres. Are they going to stop him, too? My organs may be different and I may have a deep voice, but I am a woman."

ADA HEGERBERG

When Norwegian footballer Ada Hegerberg was young, Manchester United legend Ole Gunnar Solskjær was the player Norwegian boys and girls alike looked up to. Now, the formidable striker, who holds the record for the most UEFA Champions League goals scored, is the player that kids queue for photos and signatures with.

"There was a lack of women role models when I was growing up – that's something that has changed a lot today," she told the *Guardian*. "That's very important. I can see the impact all the success that I've had with Lyon has not only had on young girls but also young boys in Norway. I feel that's a big game-changer."

Hegerberg's prowess in front of goal was evident early on. Aged 16, she became the youngest player to score a hat-trick in the Toppserien, the Norwegian league, with three goals in seven minutes. She was only 19 when she joined European champions Lyon, but she was already rated as one of the most exciting talents in Norwegian women's football. In her first season in Division 1 Féminin in France, she scored 26 goals in 22 appearances.

In December 2018 Hegerberg became the first winner of the *France Football's* Ballon d'Or Féminin after it separated from the FIFA award and finished her speech with an appeal to young girls to "believe in themselves".

"THERE WAS A LACK OF WOMEN ROLE MODELS WHEN I WAS GROWING UP."

Ada Hegerberg

There was controversy in the interview with French DJ Martin Solveig, who asked her if she knew how to twerk after winning the prestigious individual award. His question, and her curt "no", answer went viral. Hegerberg herself said it was important that "outrage is there in every situation where that theme comes up", but was keen to deflect away from that moment and instead look at what an "amazing night" it was for women in general and women who play football.

"It's a night when we celebrate the best footballers in the world, male and female," she told the *Guardian*. "They're the same as us, we've been working hard every day to achieve things like this. The mutual respect is there. There is no difference.

"That's what's so nice about nights like this because it puts both sexes up front, and that's how it should be."

Hegerberg is a big advocate for equality, and frustration at a lack of resources and support for the women's national team and grassroots girls' football in Norway led to her withdrawal from the national team in protest.

"It's a hard balance because I'm a footballer not a politician," she told the *Guardian*. "You want all the hours on the pitch to be shown, you want all the sacrifice and all the love for the game to be shown and all the great people that you have around you. I'm not here to provoke in any way. I'm just here to perform and drive the sport in the right direction. But at the same time, I am realistic about the situation we find ourselves still in, that there's so much stuff to do in order for women and young girls to get the conditions they deserve.

"It was never a quick-fix decision. I've just tried to have an impact on things for the better. At some point that can leave you with some tough choices."

As a result of her stance, Hegerberg missed out on the chance to represent her country at the 2019 FIFA Women's World Cup. The scale of the decision can perhaps be best illustrated by consideration of the

"YOU WANT ALL THE HOURS ON THE PITCH TO BE SHOWN, YOU WANT ALL THE SACRIFICE AND ALL THE LOVE FOR THE GAME TO BE SHOWN AND ALL THE GREAT PEOPLE THAT YOU HAVE AROUND YOU."

Ada Hegerberg

fact that the decision would be equivalent to players such as Lionel Messi or Cristiano Ronaldo sitting out a men's World Cup on principle.

Principles matter to Hegerberg. "I wouldn't be the player I am today if I didn't stand for my values, what I'm passionate about and what I believe in. It's easy to lose yourself on the road and you have to take some tough decisions to stay true to yourself.

"I have a lot of admiration for people who stand up for what they believe in and who actually use the voice for good. That's what I've tried to do, to stand up for what I believe is good for the women's game. I think we need to stand up together and for each other and support each other. That's why I think that Megan Rapinoe should be respected by footballers around the world, because she's taken a beating for all of us and for the game and we need strong voices like that. The more voices you have, the more impact you can leave on the sport."

MEGAN RAPINOE

On June 28, 2019, in front of a sold-out Parc de Princes crowd of 45,595 in Paris, American women's team (aka USWNT) star Megan Rapinoe shrugged off the pressure of a spat with then President Donald Trump, who had demanded she "talk the talk" after a clip of her being asked whether the USWNT would go to the White House if they won the FIFA Women's World Cup went viral.

" I'm not going to the f***ing White House," Rapinoe had quipped. With the clip released months later, on the eve of the tournament, President Trump responded with a flurry of tweets, accusing the athlete of disrespecting the country, the White House and the flag, adding: "Megan should WIN first before she TALKS! Finish the job!"

The response of Rapinoe? To score in the fifth and 65th minutes to earn the US a 2–1 win over hosts France and a place in the semi-finals. After she scored, the pink-haired forward flung her arms wide, stood still, and smiled. The image went as viral as the President's tweet.

The Redding (California)-born footballer would shine on the biggest of stages once more, despite having been a bit-part presence in the National Women's Soccer League due to injury, collecting the Golden Ball and the Golden Boot on the way to a second World Cup winners' medal.

Rapinoe had been a regular member of the US team, but her profile grew exponentially as a result of her World Cup heroics and

frank-talking manner. It would be easy for any player spotlighted in such a way, winning the Ballon d'Or and FIFA Best awards for her efforts that year, to bask in the acclaim and soak up the endorsements. Rapinoe did these things but, critically, recognized that the increased platform she had could be put to use.

On accepting her FIFA Best award, she spotlighted the anti-racism work of Raheem Sterling and Kalidou Koulibaly, the life of Iran's "Blue Girl" Sahar Khodayari, LGBTQ+ football players and more, before calling on those in the room, football's elite, to exercise their voices.

"If we really want to have meaningful change, what I think is most inspiring would be if everybody other than Sterling and Koulibaly, if they were as outraged about racism as they were, if everybody was as outraged about homophobia as the LGBTQ players, if everybody was as outraged about the lack of equal pay and investment in the women's game other than just women, that would be the most inspiring thing to me," Rapinoe said.

"That's my ask of everybody. We have such incredible opportunity, being professional football players ... we have so much success ... we have incredible platforms," she said. "I ask everybody here to lend your platform, to lift people up, to use this beautiful game to change the world for better."

Having been named *Glamour* magazine's Woman of the Year, Rapinoe used her speech to highlight the ongoing blackballing of American football star Colin Kaepernick by the NFL, who knelt during the national anthem in protest at police brutality, contrasting it to the privilege she is afforded as a white woman when it comes to speaking out. "Being white is part of the reason why it's culminating with me," she said. "The system is alive and well, so I think it's important to just say that. It's not my fault I'm benefiting but I am, so it's my responsibility to acknowledge that and to try to dismantle that system. I think it's really important to say those words, say 'white privilege', acknowledge the fact it's happening."

"LEND YOUR PLATFORM, LIFT PEOPLE UP, USE THIS BEAUTIFUL GAME TO CHANGE THE WORLD FOR THE BETTER."

Megan Rapinoe

And, in her speech after she became the fourth woman to be named as *Sports Illustrated*'s Sportsperson of the Year, she didn't hold back. "Is it truth that I'm only the fourth woman deserving of this award? I don't think so," she said.

"Is it true so few writers of colour deserve to be featured in this publication? No. Is it true so few women's voices deserve to be heard and deserve to be read in this publication? I don't think so."

Speaking out and being active around causes she is passionate about was not a new thing for Rapinoe. A gay athlete herself, she has been a big advocate of LGBTQ+ rights for years. She was one of the first players to kneel in solidarity with Kaepernick's protests in 2016. She helped raised money for those affected by the Carr wildfire that ripped through her hometown in California in 2018.

She was also a part of the six-year legal fight between USWNT players and US Soccer for the right to equal pay and bonuses with the US Men's National Team, which has concluded with a $24 million settlement reached.

"We feel like this is a huge win – obviously contingent upon the ratification of the CBA [collective bargaining agreement] – but it will have equal pay on everything moving forward," she told *The Athletic*.

"It's honestly kind of surreal. I feel like I need to take a step back. We've all been in the trenches of it for so long. I think I honestly don't even understand how monumental this is."

Turning 37 in July 2022, Rapinoe is reaching the twilight of her playing career. Her talent gave her fame, but her greatest legacy will be the example she has set in how athletes can use their voice for good.

SUZANN PETTERSEN

On August 13, 2019, Catriona Matthew selected Norwegian golfer Suzann Pettersen as one of her four captain's choices for Europe's Solheim Cup team to take on the USA in the biennial international competition. It was a bold move, given Pettersen was ranked 620th in the world, and Matthew received much criticism for it.

The 38-year-old had spent two years away from the sport on maternity leave and had played just two events prior to selection. Two months later, on September 15 at the Gleneagles PGA Centenary Course in Scotland, Pettersen, the last European player on the course, holed a birdie putt on the 18th and final hole to win the match one-up and, with it, the Solheim Cup for Europe 14–13. If the hole had been halved, the match would likewise have ended in a half-point to each team and Team USA would have retained the Cup.

"I think this is a perfect closure," Pettersen said shortly after announcing her retirement. "A nice 'the end' for [my] professional career. It doesn't get any better. Life's changed so much for me over the last year. He's [son Herman] obviously the biggest thing that's ever happened for me. But now I know what it feels like to win as a mom. I'm going to leave it like that."

When Pettersen retired she had won 15 LPGA titles – including the 2007 Women's PGA Championship, by one stroke over Australian Karrie Webb, and the 2013 Evian Championship, beating Korean-born New Zealander Lydia Ko by two strokes – and six times on the European Tour. She was a five-time Norwegian Amateur Champion, and won the Girls Amateur Championship at High Post, Salisbury, England, in 1999, before she turned professional in September 2000 at the age of 19.

In 2015, her insatiable desire to win sparked controversy when, during the Solheim Cup in St Leon-Rot in Baden-Württemberg in Germany, Pettersen disputed US golfer Alison Lee's assumption that the next putt had been conceded. Lee had picked up the ball after her missed putt before the European four-ball pair of Pettersen and Charley Hull had conceded. Pettersen insisted the shot had not been conceded, which meant Team Europe won that hole. Her own team captain Carin Koch and assistant captain Annika Sörenstam tried to convince her to change her mind and concede but they could not retrospectively change the outcome. Europe won that match, but the US would go on to win the Cup on the last day.

Despite her successful career, in which she reached a personal-best ranking of World No. 2 a number of times, it was her Solheim Cup-winning putt in 2019 – seven years after she was last ranked in the top two – that helped exorcize the ghost of the 2015 controversy.

In retirement, she is using her profile to champion environmental issues and sustainability. "As a mother of a young child, it is incredible how concerned you become over the future of the planet, its biodiversity, air quality and climate. These things are absolutely vital to the health and wellbeing of future generations, so we all need to do our best to make things better," she told Sky Sports.

"When you think about golf, you think golf is such a great arena, it's green, it's outdoors, it's fresh air. But there's a lot that goes into maintaining a golf course ... there's water, you have all the chemicals, so if you start looking at how the golf course can harm nature, it's quite a lot actually."

Using her voice is important to her. "I definitely think the life of a top athlete has changed and there's a lot more awareness of trying to use the platform that you've been given, to speak your word and the world will listen," she said. "So, I think it's a great opportunity for athletes to speak their mind, in whatever topic that might be, because the world has changed a lot over the last 10 to 15 years – you have social media, you have so many channels, you can communicate, you can deliver messages."

Now a mother of two, Pettersen returned to golf to be one of Matthew's assistant captains in the victorious 2021 Solheim Cup team at the Inverness Club in Toledo, Ohio, and will be captain for 2023, at Finca Cortesin in Andalucia, Spain. "It's been a part of our lives for so many years," she told the Golf Channel of her return to the Solheim Cup in 2021. "I must say, it's something that feels very natural."

In the European team room at Inverness there was a poster of Pettersen's 2019 Solheim Cup-winning putt from 2019.

"Walking past it every day I just look at it and I'm like, 'Wow, that's so cool'," said Finland's European rookie Matilda Castren. "I hope that I can be there one day making that winning putt."

"I DEFINITELY THINK THE LIFE OF A TOP ATHLETE HAS CHANGED AND THERE'S A LOT MORE AWARENESS OF TRYING TO USE THE PLATFORM THAT YOU'VE BEEN GIVEN, TO SPEAK YOUR WORD AND THE WORLD WILL LISTEN."

Suzann Pettersen

BRIGID KOSGEI

"When I think back to my humble beginnings and the challenges we went through growing up, I tell myself I cannot go back to that life and it pushes me to do well," Brigid Kosgei told the BBC in 2019.

Raised by her mother in Elgeyo-Marakwet county in Kenya, a region known for producing top runners, Kosgei was one of seven children. Her school was 10km from her home, so she often had to run to avoid being late. "On my way I met athletes who were training and said to myself: 'I can be like them,'" she said.

Gradually, she began to take part in middle-distance events at school but, at 18. she left school in 2012 to focus on running after her school fees became prohibitive for her mother.

"By the time I was in form three, the arrears were over $1,500 (£1,200). My mother tried to convince me to stay on by saying she would borrow the money but I told her: 'For how long will we keep borrowing?'" she said.

Training with her soon-to-be husband Mathew, Kosgei took a break to have twins but she resumed training in 2015 and joined a training camp.

"My husband told me not to worry – he would take care of the children – and that I should just focus on my career and soon the

"ON MY WAY I MET ATHLETES WHO WERE TRAINING AND SAID TO MYSELF: 'I CAN BE LIKE THEM.'"

Brigid Kosgei

children also got used to seeing me only on the weekends when I'd return home," said Kosgei.

In November 2015 Kosgei ran in her first marathon at Porto in Portugal and she finished first with a four-minute lead over her nearest rival. It was an amazing start to a marathon career, which saw her finish in the top two in eight of her first nine races: after winning in Milan in April 2016, she finished second to Sarah Chepchirchir at the Lisbon Marathon in 2016 in a personal best time of 2:24.45 and won the Honolulu Marathon in 2016 and 2017 – the latter breaking the course record by more than five minutes. A personal best time of 2:20.22 was good enough only for second place behind Tirunesh Dibaba at the 2017 race at Chicago. The following year she was second at the London Marathon behind Vivian Cheruiyot and won the Chicago Marathon, both times setting personal best times.

Kosgei set the world alight in 2019, first by becoming the youngest woman to win the London Marathon with the third-best time ever, then by breaking the world record in Chicago, with a time of 2:14.04, 81 seconds faster than Paula Radcliffe's London Marathon victory in 2003, and her own personal best by more than four minutes. A day earlier, another Kenyan, Eliud Kipchoge, had broken the two-hour barrier for the 26.2-mile distance in Vienna, but his time was not recognized as a world record because it did not meet race criteria.

It took four months for Kosgei's record to be ratified by World Athletics. "I kept saying, 'Tomorrow is my day,'" she said. "I wanted to be the second Kipchoge – the Kipchoge for women. I focused on that.

"I was not expecting [the world record]. I was expecting to run 2:16 or 2:17. It's amazing to run 2:14, but the world record was in my head. When I started the race, I was thinking I need 2:15 for Paula's record.

"People were cheering, 'you are running the world record! World record!'" she said. "I felt their energy, and they inspired me.

"I CONTINUED TO FOLLOW MY GUIDING PRINCIPLES OF HARD WORK, DISCIPLINE AND PERSEVERANCE; THAT'S ALL I CAN DO AND THEN HOPE THAT'S ENOUGH FOR A GREAT PERFORMANCE ON RACE DAY."

Brigid Kosgei

"I like some spectators around to cheer you, they motivate so with the spectators and people running with you it gives you morale when you are running with them and I like running with them."

After a pandemic pause, Kosgei returned to London to win the rescheduled 2020 London Marathon by more than three minutes, having broken clear of the leading pack 18 miles into the race. She appeared at her first Olympics, the delayed 2020 Tokyo Games, where she finished second behind fellow Kenyan Peres Jepchirchir. Two months later, she finished fourth in London before winning the delayed Tokyo Marathon in a third fastest ever time of 2:16.20.

"Once I was back to training [following the pandemic], it was business as usual, getting in my miles and just trying to be the best version of myself," she told *Vogue* magazine. "I continued to follow my guiding principles of hard work, discipline and perseverance; that's all I can do and then hope that's enough for a great performance on race day."

SAHAR KHODAYARI

Football is not just a game, it is so much more and, for some, it's life and death. For millions of women across the world, football represents a rebellion against societal expectations, stereotypes and, in some cases, legal systems.

In Iran women have been banned from watching football alongside men for more than 40 years. The process for them to be banned from stadiums was not a formal one, but a creeping change as the political Islamist policies of the Ayatollah Khomeini absorbed the 1979 revolution and gave birth to the Islamic Republic of Iran. Universities were closed for three years after the revolution as the Republic clamped down and were only reopened under Islamic supervision. Almost two years after the revolution, wearing the hijab became mandatory. And, as political Islam took hold and stretched its tentacles through Iranian society, women vanished from football.

For close to 15 years, women have protested the unofficial ban and attempted to circumvent the rules through the Open Stadiums movement, which was founded in 2005 when a group of women football fans protested outside the country's national stadium during a 2005 World Cup qualification match between Iran and Bahrain.

In 2006, the Iranian film director Jafar Panahi released a film, *Offside*, inspired by the efforts of his own daughter, who decided to attend a game despite the risks involved.

In recent years, the pressure has been building on Iran to allow women to enter stadiums and watch alongside men, but the country's leaders have been resistant. The arguments, to safeguard women from men and

their profanities, are outdated, but the issue has come to represent more. Give women this concession and what else will they want?

"They think that, if they give up on this, it's a noose for them," Maryam Shojaei, the sister of Iran national football team captain Masoud Shojaei told the *Guardian* in August 2019. "People will ask for more. If they give in in one area, they fear they will have to give in in others."

In June 2019, with frustrations building, the FIFA president, Gianni Infantino, wrote a letter to the Iranian FA president, Mehdi Taj, describing the decision to not allow women into a game that month, having previously permitted a small group of female fans to attend a match in Tehran's Azadi stadium in November 2018, as "disappointing".

The letter read: "This is not in line with the commitments given to us in March 2018 by [Iran's] president Rouhani when we were assured that important progress would be made on this matter soon.

"Whilst we are aware of the challenges and cultural sensitivities, we simply have to continue making progress here, not only because we owe it to women all over the world, but also because we have a responsibility to do so, under the most basic principles set out in the FIFA statutes.

"In the circumstances I would be very grateful if you could inform FIFA, at your earliest convenience but no later than 15 July 2019, as to the concrete steps which both the FFIRI [Football Federation Islamic Republic of Iran] and the Iranian state authorities will now be taking in order to ensure that all Iranian and foreign women who wish to do so will be allowed to buy tickets and to attend the matches of the qualifiers for the FIFA World Cup Qatar 2022, which will start in September 2019."

However, the July 15 deadline passed without comment from FFIRI.

On September 2, 2019, though, the movement was thrust into the spotlight globally. Having attempted to attend a game at the Azadi stadium in Tehran in mid-March, wearing a blue wig and long coat to disguise herself as a man, 29-year-old Sahar Khodayari was arrested.

AFTER SEVEN DAYS IN HOSPITAL WITH BURNS OVER 90 PER CENT OF HER BODY, KHODAYARI'S DEATH AND BURIAL UNDER TIGHT SECURITY WAS ANNOUNCED.

After hearing that she faced six months in jail for her efforts, the Esteghlal FC fan, which wears blue, doused herself in petrol and set herself ablaze outside the court she had been summoned to attend after being charged.

After seven days in hospital with burns over 90 per cent of her body, Khodayari's death and burial under tight security was announced.

Through her devastating action Khodayari, nicknamed the "Blue Girl", ramped up the pressure from FIFA on the Iranian authorities.

"We are aware of that tragedy and deeply regret it," a FIFA statement said. "FIFA convey our condolences to the family and friends of Sahar and reiterate our calls on the Iranian authorities to ensure the freedom and safety of any women engaged in this legitimate fight to end the stadium ban for women in Iran."

Masoud Shojaei, whose sister has only been able to watch him play in away games, said on Instagram that the ban is "rooted in outdated and cringe-worthy thoughts that will not be understood by future generations."

In October 2019 it was reported that Iran had lifted the ban and allowed women to attend the country's World Cup qualifier against Cambodia. However, only 3,500 tickets were allocated to women fans and, despite swathes of empty seats, they had to enter through a separate entrance and were sat penned together in cages separating them from male fans.

These conditions were similarly in place when around 2,000 women were allowed into the Azadi stadium in January 2022 to watch Iran beat Iraq 1–0 to qualify for the 2022 World Cup in Qatar.

NAOMI OSAKA

"I'm writing this to say I'm not going to do any press during Roland Garros," said the then world No. 2 Naomi Osaka ahead of the French Open in May 2021.

"I've often felt that people have no regard for athletes' mental health and this rings true whenever I see a press conference or partake in one."

The backlash the four-time Grand Slam winner received was vicious. The French Tennis Federation president Gilles Moretton confirmed that the organization would penalize her for refusing to take part in press conferences and the four Grand Slam tournaments issued a joint statement on the controversy. She was fined $15,000 by the French Open for not speaking to the media after her first-round match with Patricia Maria Ţig and was warned she faced expulsion if she continued her silence. So, she pulled out.

The response was hard line, yet the message from Osaka was clear: this was not about the press, this was "nothing personal to the tournament, or anything against most journalists. I have a friendly relationship with most of them." This was a young woman struggling with anxiety and bouts of depression articulating herself.

It was incredibly brave. Here was someone on one of the world's biggest sporting stages not just sharing #itsOKtonotbeOK messages but exposing their own vulnerabilities and trying to tackle some of the causes they had identified. Traditionally, sports stars have tried to present themselves as superhuman, infallible and unbreakable in a bid to avoid any

chance of exposing a weakness. Here, Osaka was owning her identity.

"Anyone that knows me knows I'm introverted, and anyone that has seen me at the tournaments will notice that I'm often wearing headphones as that helps dull my social anxiety," Osaka wrote when announcing she would not be competing further. She explained she suffers from "huge waves of anxiety" before speaking with the press.

"So here in Paris I was already feeling vulnerable and anxious, so I thought it was better to exercise selfcare and skip the press conferences. I announced it pre-emptively because I do feel like the rules are quite outdated in parts and I wanted to highlight that."

Instead of criticism, there should have been understanding and reflection by the tennis world and the media. This was the opportunity for a thoughtful discussion on the role, format and context of press conferences, which have changed very little over the years, and on the mental toll of tournament tennis, the health of players and the best way of managing that. Instead, the response was essentially: "get in line or get out".

The support for Osaka came from far and wide too, not least from athletes who understand the pressures of top-level competitive sport. "Stay strong. I admire your vulnerability," wrote Coco Gauff.

"It's incredibly brave that Naomi Osaka has revealed her truth about her struggle with depression," said Billie Jean King. "Right now, the important thing is that we give her the space and time she needs. We wish her well."

Osaka was born in Japan to a Japanese mother and Haitian father but moved to the US with her family when she was three to live with her paternal grandparents. Naomi and her sister Mari were coached by their father, Leonard François, who had been inspired by the story of the Williams sisters and their father, Richard. Osaka started to turn heads when she beat former US Open champion Samantha Stosur in her WTA Tour debut in 2014 but it was in 2018, when she won her first WTA title at the Indian Wells Open, that she was catapulted onto the main stage. At the US Open that year, Osaka became the first Japanese player to win a Grand Slam title when she defeated Serena Williams, but an argument between Williams and the umpire soured the match. With Williams given a game penalty, Serena had lost the first set when she received a code violation for being coached, then a second one after smashing her racquet. At a changeover, trailing 4–3 in the second set, Williams got into another argument with the umpire and was assessed a game penalty, making it 5–3. Boos rained down in the direction of the umpire during the match, which ended 6–4 to Osaka, and the awards ceremony – what should have been a hugely significant moment for Osaka – lost its shine and she was in tears as she received the trophy. In many respects that moment likely influenced her difficulties with the media. Williams tried to turn the attentions of the frustrated crowd by praising the young new champion but questions about the incident would stalk Osaka for months.

Her decision to speak out about her mental health struggles and to step back from press conferences was not the first time Osaka had used her platform to highlight issues that resonate far beyond sport. In her 2020 runs at the Cincinnati Open and to a second US Open title, Osaka used the stage to show her support for the Black Lives Matter movement. She planned to withdraw before the Ohio semi-final after the police shooting of the 29-year-old Jacob Blake in Wisconsin but played on after the organizers postponed the competition for a day in support of her stance. At the US Open, she stepped onto the court before each of her seven matches wearing black facemasks bearing the name of a different Black person killed without consequence, many by the police, emblazoned across them in white lettering.

Osaka is not alone. She is one of many young, empowered women athletes to have embraced the platform their talent has given them and is part of a new generation of female athlete activists who are not only fighting for their rights within sport but also tackling many of the broader issues in society. In doing so, at the age of 24 – at the start of 2022 – and with so much more to give, Osaka has inspired others to do the same, provoked conversations on race, mental health, sexism and protest and challenged the status quo.

ALLYSON FELIX

Allyson Felix is the most decorated American track and field Olympian of all time, with 11 medals (seven golds, three silvers and a bronze) across five Games, one more than Carl Lewis, but it is the legacy of her battle for the rights of athlete mothers that means more.

Having decided she wanted to start a family, Felix knew she was taking a risk. "For most of my life, I was focused on one thing: winning medals. And I was good at it. At 32, I was one of the most decorated athletes in history: a six-time Olympic gold medal winner and an 11-time world champion. But last year, my focus expanded: I wanted to be a professional athlete and a mother. In some ways, that dream was crazy," she told the *New York Times*.

"I decided to start a family in 2018 knowing that pregnancy can be 'the kiss of death' in my industry, as the runner Phoebe Wright put it in the *New York Times* last week. It was a terrifying time for me because I was negotiating a renewal of my Nike contract, which had ended in December 2017."

With nine Olympic medals to her name, it would be easy to assume that the sportswear giant would

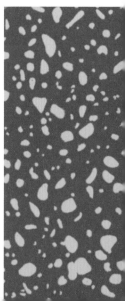

"FOR MOST OF MY LIFE, I WAS FOCUSED ON ONE THING: WINNING MEDALS. AND I WAS GOOD AT IT."

Allyson Felix

have been keen to renew the deal. Instead, Nike wanted to pay her 70 per cent less than she had been paid before, and she felt "pressure to return to form as soon as possible" after the birth of daughter Camryn, despite suffering from life-threatening pre-eclampsia, which meant she had to undergo an emergency caesarean at 32 weeks.

"I asked Nike to contractually guarantee that I wouldn't be punished if I didn't perform at my best in the months surrounding childbirth. I wanted to set a new standard. If I, one of Nike's most widely marketed athletes, couldn't secure these protections, who could?"

Nike declined and in 2019 Felix spoke publicly about it. On August 12, less than three months later, Nike announced it was introducing a new maternity policy for all sponsored athletes. It included a guarantee that a pregnant athlete's pay would not be cut for 18 months around the pregnancy. As a result, a number of other sponsors changed their terms too.

"When I think about the world that Cammy will grow up in, I don't want her – or any other woman or girl – to have to fight the battles that I fought," Felix told CNBC.

"It's really hard to balance being a mom and a professional athlete, and the reality is that there's a certain level of financial support and security that's necessary to be able to do it," she added.

"There has always been a silence and a fear surrounding motherhood in sports. I remember feeling like I had to choose between this sport that I love and my family."

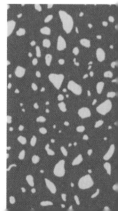

"I WANTED TO SET A NEW STANDARD. IF I, ONE OF NIKE'S MOST WIDELY MARKETED ATHLETES, COULDN'T SECURE THESE PROTECTIONS, WHO COULD?"

Allyson Felix

Instead, Felix signed a contract with Athleta, and she worked with the clothing brand and the Women's Sports Foundation to create a grant to help fund childcare costs for travelling athletes. The first six recipients were given $10,000 each to help them compete at the delayed Tokyo Games.

In Tokyo, Felix claimed bronze in the 400m and gold in the 4 x 400m. After the Games, she posted a poignant black and white image of herself with some of the medals from her career hanging around her neck above her exposed caesarean scar.

In addition to fighting for the rights of athlete mothers, Felix has used her platform to highlight the pregnancy-related issues Black women face, with pre-eclampsia and eclampsia 60 per cent more common in Black women.

"I wasn't fully aware of the Black maternal mortality crisis in America," she told lifestyle website Hello Giggles. "If I could do something so that other women wouldn't be in the same situation, or would at least be more prepared, then I wanted to take part [in that]."

BECKY
HAMMON

In 2014 Becky Hammon became the second woman to be an assistant coach in the NBA and the first to do so full-time. In 2020 she became the first female interim head coach after San Antonio Spurs head coach Gregg Popovich was ejected from a game against the LA Lakers.

H ammon's journey through the women's game into the men's and back again has been a long one. The former player began dribbling basketballs with her family when she was quite young and played in high school in her hometown of Rapid City, South Dakota. In her senior year she averaged 26 points, four rebounds and five steals per game. At five foot six, Hammon did not attract big college recruiters, but she joined Colorado State University and played for the Colorado State Rams. She was a prolific scorer, named the Western Athletic Conference Mountain Division player of the year in 1998–99, and broke record after record at Colorado State, including a career points tally of 2,740, 21.92 points per game, 918 field goals, 539 successful free throws. The University retired her number 25 jersey at the end of her college career.

Despite her college form, no team selected her in the 1999 WNBA Draft, but she signed as a free agent with New York Liberty that summer.

In 2007 Hammon was traded to the San Antonio Silver Stars. From the moment she signed she caught the eye of Popovich, who was impressed by her. As the *New Yorker* magazine wrote: "Though only five feet six, Hammon was a commanding presence on the court:

gum-snapping, energetic, her quick cuts and jab steps to the basket punctuated by a swishing ponytail. She could slip through a narrow space between two defenders and drive to the hoop, scooping a shot that would skim the rim and slide through the net. Like Magic Johnson, she flipped no-look passes over her shoulder, and, like Stephen Curry, she hit shots from half-court."

What had most impressed one of the most respected basketball coaches in the game though was her leadership on the court. "I'd watch the game, and the only thing I could see – it's an exaggeration, I mean, but – was Becky's aura, her leadership, her effect on teammates, her effect on the crowd, the way she handled herself," Popovich added in the same story. "She was, like, the ultimate leader. Energy, juice, vitality. At the same time, she was doing intelligent things on the court, making decisions that mattered."

On a flight from London back to the US after the London 2012 Olympic Games, where she had competed for Russia having not been selected for the US, Hammon chatted the whole way with Popovich after they had bumped into each other and, by the end of their conversation, he was considering offering her a job.

An ACL tear in a 2013 game against the Los Angeles Sparks ended Hammon's playing career and she approached Popovich about sitting in on some Spurs practice sessions. By the summer of 2014 Hammon was hired as an assistant to Popovich. "It has nothing to do with her being a woman. She happens to be a woman," Popovich said.

Her reputation grew quickly. Pau Gasol said in a piece with the *Players' Tribune*: "I've played with some of the best players of this generation … and I've played under two of the sharpest minds in the history of sports, in Phil Jackson and Gregg Popovich. And I'm telling you: Becky Hammon can coach. I'm not saying she can coach pretty

"SHE WAS THE ULTIMATE LEADER. ENERGY, JUICE, VITALITY. AT THE SAME TIME, SHE WAS DOING INTELLIGENT THINGS ON THE COURT, MAKING DECISIONS THAT MATTERED."

Gregg Popovich

well. I'm not saying she can coach enough to get by. I'm not saying she can coach almost at the level of the NBA's male coaches. I'm saying: Becky Hammon can coach NBA basketball. Period."

In 2015, she became the first ever female head coach in the NBA Summer League with the Spurs and she won the Las Vegas Summer League title.

In December 2021, after eight seasons in the NBA, it was reported that the trailblazer was returning to the WNBA, signing a five-year deal to lead the Las Vegas Aces, formerly her team, the San Antonio Silver Stars.

"My heart was saying it was time to go. This is where I am supposed to be right now," she said in a phone interview with the Associated Press. "There were a lot of sleepless nights getting to this conclusion.

"Las Vegas sees me as a head coach now. The WNBA has called every year with job openings. … I've always said thank you, I'm very flattered but stayed on this path. This was the first time where I was like, I'll listen."

LAUREL HUBBARD

"I'm not here to change the world, I just want to be me and do what I do," said weightlifter Laurel Hubbard in 2017, the year in which she first competed as a female weightlifter. Except, just by wanting to be herself and do what she does she has changed the world and become a powerful role model in the process.

Hubbard's selection for the delayed 2020 Tokyo Olympics made her the first ever transgender athlete to compete in an individual sport – where Canada's women's national team player Quinn became the first out, transgender and non-binary athlete to win an Olympic gold.

Hubbard competed in domestic men's competitions as a junior and was the New Zealand national record holder, before stepping away from the sport aged 23 in 2001.

"It just became too much to bear ... the pressure of trying to fit into a world that perhaps wasn't really set up for people like myself," she said more recently.

In 2012, Hubbard came out as transgender and began hormone therapy. In 2017 she competed in international weightlifting for the first time since transitioning, having re-embraced the sport she had fallen out of love with.

She won a gold medal at the Australian International and Australian Open in Melbourne competing in the heaviest category, +90kg. She also won two silver medals at the IWF World Weightlifting Championships in Anaheim, California, that year too.

Right from the start of her return to the sport, Hubbard faced criticism for competing against women who were born as women, even though she met all eligibility requirements. Despite the furore, which included fellow competitors and other national federations, she continued to compete, avoiding talking openly to the media about the storm that followed her.

"People believe what they believe when they are shown something that may be new and different to what they know. It's instinctive to be defensive," she said in 2017.

"It's not really my job to change what they think, what they feel and what they believe. I just hope they look at the bigger picture, rather than just trusting whatever their gut may have told them."

Hubbard was leading at the 2018 Commonwealth Games when she had to withdraw because of an elbow injury but went on to win two gold medals at the Pacific Games in Samoa in 2019, this after considering retirement from the sport a year earlier.

The International Olympic Committee had changed its rules to allow transgender athletes to compete as a woman if their testosterone levels were below a certain threshold in 2015.

Hubbard met all the requirements to compete at the Tokyo Olympics on June 21, 2021 and was backed by her federation.

"As well as being among the world's best for her event, Laurel has met the IWF eligibility criteria, including those based on IOC Consensus Statement guidelines for transgender athletes," said New Zealand Olympic Committee chief executive Kereyn Smith.

"We acknowledge that gender identity in sport is a highly sensitive and complex issue requiring a balance between human rights and fairness on the field of play," he added.

"As the New Zealand team, we have a strong culture of 'manaaki' (respect) and inclusion and respect for all."

In Tokyo, with the eyes of the world on her, Hubbard made Olympic history in Tokyo but she failed to register a successful lift after one attempt at 120kg and two at 125kg.

She said afterwards: "I know that from a sporting perspective I haven't really hit the standards that I put upon myself and perhaps the standards that my country has expected of me.

"But one of the things for which I am profoundly grateful is that the supporters in New Zealand have given me so much and have been beyond astonishing.

"I'd like to thank the New Zealand Olympic Committee – they have supported me through what have been quite difficult times.

"I know that my participation at these Games has not been entirely without controversy, but they have been just so wonderful and I'm so grateful to them."

Hubbard didn't manage to complete a successful lift in Japan, but she lifted the aspirations of trans athletes and that was the bigger prize.

"I KNOW THAT MY PARTICIPATION AT THESE GAMES HAS NOT BEEN ENTIRELY WITHOUT CONTROVERSY BUT THEY HAVE BEEN JUST SO WONDERFUL AND I'M SO GRATEFUL TO THEM."

Laurel Hubbard

TATYANA MCFADDEN

"I've always had a determined mindset," Tatyana McFadden told CNBC ahead of the Covid-delayed 2020 Tokyo Olympic Games. She has needed it. McFadden, widely believed to be the fastest female wheelchair racer of all time, was born in Leningrad – now St Petersburg – in Russia with spina bifida which left her paralyzed from the waist down.

D octors didn't expect her to live for more than a few days and her parents abandoned her and she ended up in a local orphanage, where she lived for the first six years of her life – without medical support or basic provisions for her disability, even a wheelchair. She learned to walk on her hands to keep up with other children in the orphanage, which built up a strength in her arms that would power her to an extraordinary athletics career.

Tatyana's fortunes turned when she was adopted by the commissioner of disabilities for the US Department of Health and Human Services, Debbie McFadden and her partner Bridget O'Shaughnessy. McFadden met the six-year-old when visiting "Orphanage No. 13" on a business trip. The couple adopted Tatyana and brought her back to their home in Ellicott City, Maryland. Her adopting parents enrolled her in various sports programmes to strengthen her muscles and she experimented with several sports through the adaptive sports programme the Bennett Blazers, but it was wheelchair racing that captured her heart.

"The moment I sat in that racing chair, I knew it was for me. It was something that I never felt before – freedom,"

she said in the documentary *Rising Phoenix*.

She broke the world record for the 100 metres sprint in her age group at 13 years old and began to turn heads. McFadden competed in her first Paralympic Games, aged 15, at Athens in 2004, after travelling to California for the Paralympic trials. She qualified in four events in Athens and won two medals in the T54 event, a silver in the 100 metres and bronze in the 200m.

She was celebrated on her return to Atholton High School and was included in the homecoming parade. However, she was banned from competing alongside non-wheelchair athletes on her school track team by the Athletic Director and Principal. They considered her racing wheelchair to be a safety hazard and it gave her an unfair advantage. She was forced to compete separately, circling empty tracks with no one else to compete against. However, Deborah McFadden knew the law; she had helped to write the Americans with Disabilities Act of 1990 and McFadden's exclusion from her high school's track team races was in breach of the law. When deciding whether to sue, Tatyana McFadden considered the wider impact on those who would come after her, including her sister, who was adopted from Albania and had a leg amputated above the knee. "She was in elementary school at the time," Tatyana said in an interview with *Women's Running*. "I didn't want her to go through the same experience of having to fight for this, to be treated the way I was treated.

"I was like, 'Well, I'm just gonna do it. What's the worst thing that can happen? Nothing bad will come out when you're trying to do something good, to push for these things.'"

The impact of the case was brutal. When a federal judge issued an injunction which allowed her to race, parents booed the young athlete for suing the Howard County Public School System. Eventually the County conceded, and McFadden was allowed to race, although her performances did not earn competition points for her school team. The impact of her stand was huge. The Maryland Fitness and Athletics Equity for Students with Disabilities Act became state law and was nicknamed "Tatyana's Law". That law inspired national legislation in 2013.

The fight gave McFadden a new purpose; she wanted to continue to use her voice but she needed the sporting platform to be able to do that. "When I was 15, I thought to myself, 'Well, if I want people to listen to me, I just need to be the best,'" she said to *Women's Running*. "If you look at the Williams sisters or Michael Jordan or Michael Johnson – the greatest athletes in history – they became the best and people listened. I thought the same: I need to win everything."

She won gold and silver sprint medals at the 2006 World Championships in Assen and then, after graduating, travelled to Beijing for the 2008 Paralympics Games, where she won silver medals in the 200, 400 and 800 metres and a bronze in the 4 x 100 metres relay

McFadden took on her first marathon in Chicago in 2009 and won. She then did the same in New York in 2010, Chicago and London in 2011, Boston, Chicago, London and New York in 2013, London in 2014 and Boston and New York in 2015, where she broke the women's course record by seven minutes and 20 seconds.

The summer Paralympic Games were not enough for her, so McFadden competed at the Winter Paralympic Games in Sochi in 2014, and won a silver medal in cross-country skiing in front of her family, including her biological mother. "The most important part is just having my family here. It's definitely a fulfilling moment," she told the BBC.

She has since won the London and Boston Marathons in 2016, the Chicago Marathon in 2017, Boston in 2018 and Chicago again in 2021.

McFadden also won three gold medals at the London 2012 Paralympics and four golds and two silvers at Rio in 2016. She competed at her sixth Paralympic Games, in the delayed event at Tokyo in 2021, and collected a gold medal in the mixed 4 x 100 metres, 800m silver and 5,000m bronze. Her impact though, goes far beyond the medals.

STÉPHANIE FRAPPART

Stéphanie Frappart has walked a path few others have managed, refereeing at the top level of women's and men's football. Frappart has been a FIFA-listed referee since 2009 and began refereeing in the men's French third division, the Championnat National, in 2011. On the international stage, she has officiated at the 2015 FIFA Women's World Cup, 2016 Rio Olympic Games and 2017 UEFA Women's European Championship.

She became the first woman to referee in men's Ligue 2 in 2014 and stepped up to the top division in France, Ligue 1, on April 28, 2019 in a game between SC Amiens and RC Strasbourg. "I started refereeing in Ligue 1 last season, taking charge of two games," Frappart said in an interview with the FIFA.com website. "It was a huge recognition of my abilities and hard work. It was also a way of showing every young girl that it's possible to reach that level if you work hard and give yourself the means to get there."

That year was a breakthrough year for the woman considered the best female referee in the world. After refereeing in the top tier domestically, she was selected to officiate at the FIFA Women's World Cup in France and refereed the final between the US and the Netherlands. Prior to the final she took charge of three games, a 0–0 group stage draw between Argentina and Japan, the Netherlands' 2–1 win over Canada and Sweden's 2–1 quarter-final defeat of Germany.

"It's a huge source of pride to be appointed for this match because I represent all of the referees at this World Cup," she said. "It's a major recognition. It's impossible to describe my emotions because we've all been working for several years to get here, a bit like the players.

"Our preparations began just after Canada 2015. We had seminars, training courses and a preparation programme focusing on fitness, tactics and technique. In terms of fitness, we had trainers working with us throughout the year and even during the tournament. We also went through all the preparations for the use of VAR."

Less than a month after the final on July 7, it was announced that Frappart would become the first woman to referee in a major men's European match, by taking charge of the 2019 UEFA Super Cup between Champions League winners, Liverpool, and Europa League winners, Chelsea. The response from the players was emphatic.

"I think gender is irrelevant. If the quality is there, and obviously it is there, because otherwise she wouldn't get appointed for this game, then it doesn't really matter," said Liverpool captain Virgil van Dijk. "If you look at her CV as well, she had been doing so many good games and, you know, they made probably the right decision. And what I said before, gender doesn't matter at all."

The then Chelsea manager Frank Lampard added: "It's great news. I'm very pleased to be a part of this moment in history, which is very much due. I think the game has come on a long way in many ways in terms of the Women's World Cup that we all watched this summer, in terms of how much respect the game's getting, how many people are watching, the interest in the game. I think we were slow everywhere on this and now we're trying to make strides, and there's still a long way to go. It's a huge moment. It should be very well addressed, and we are pleased it's a historical moment and it's one more step in the right direction."

On November 11 she was named as the referee for the inaugural Champions Cup, between the league winners of the Northern Ireland Football League Premiership, Linfield, and the League of Ireland Premier Division, Dundalk.

Another record was set in 2020, when she became the

"IT'S A HUGE SOURCE OF PRIDE TO BE APPOINTED FOR THIS MATCH BECAUSE I REPRESENT ALL OF THE REFEREES AT THIS WORLD CUP. IT'S A MAJOR RECOGNITION."

Stéphanie Frappart

first woman to officiate in a men's UEFA Champions League match, overseeing Juventus's game with Dynamo Kyiv. In March 2021 she was in action in the women's UEFA Champions League for the meeting between Atletico Madrid and Chelsea. In the same month she became the first woman to officiate a men's FIFA World Cup qualifier, taking charge of a game between the Netherlands and Latvia. Pierluigi Collina, the chairman of FIFA's Referees Committee, oversaw the appointments of match officials and he told the FIFA. com website: "Although they already had some matches in important men's competitions under their belts, officiating a FIFA World Cup qualifier for the first time is special and is something to be very proud of.

"They have worked very hard in recent years and these appointments are recognition for the good job that they have done.

"FIFA will continue to champion the development of female refereeing and I'm confident that the appointment of female match officials to men's games will be absolutely commonplace in the future."

SIMONE BILES

In the team final of the women's gymnastics at the delayed 2020 Tokyo Olympic Games, Simone Biles's grip in what was for her usually routine Yurchenko vault, with 2.5 twists, slipped. She reverted to 1.5 twists and stumbled on landing to protect herself from injury. The shock around the auditorium in the Ariake Gymnastics Centre was palpable.

Biles, who had dominated the all-around, floor and team events for eight years, left the hall with USA Gymnastics staff, returned, spoke to her teams and then her withdrawal was announced. When asked why the most decorated gymnast of all time had chosen to step back, the reply was simple: "To focus on my wellbeing. There is more to life than just gymnastics." She explained that she had experienced "the twisties", a phrase used to describe the feeling of losing all spatial awareness while in the air.

Later she reflected further on her decision to sit out a number of events, before returning to compete in the beam final, performing a scaled-back routine for which she still won a bronze medal.

"I don't trust myself as much as I used to," she said. "I don't know if it's age and I'm a little bit more nervous when I do gymnastics. I feel like I'm also not having as much fun. This Olympic Games, I wanted it to be for myself, but I came in and I felt like I was still doing it for other people. It hurts my heart that doing what I love has been kind of taken away from me to please other people."

And in the coming months, she admitted that she should have stepped away long before the Games. She pointed to recent events which had taken a huge

"I DON'T TRUST MYSELF AS MUCH AS I USED TO."

Simone Biles

toll on her: the trial of team doctor Larry Nassar for sexual abuse; being the last remaining survivor from that team; and representing an organization which had failed to protect her for so many years. "If you looked at everything I've gone through for the past seven years, I should have never made another Olympic team," she told *New York Magazine*. "I should have quit way before Tokyo, when Larry Nassar was in the media for two years. It was too much.

"But I was not going to let him take something I've worked for since I was six years old. I wasn't going to let him take that joy away from me. So, I pushed past that for as long as my mind and my body would let me."

Having captured four gold medals at the 2016 Rio Games (in the vault, beam, team and all-around) and 32 Olympic and World Championship medals in all, Biles prizes her bronze medal from the beam event in Tokyo above all others because of what it represents:

a rejection of the "win at all costs" mentality. That the gymnast was named *TIME* magazine's Athlete of the Year and won the BBC's lifetime achievement award in the year she won the fewest medals speaks to her contribution to the shifting narrative around the mental wellbeing of athletes.

Biles pointed to Naomi Osaka, who was returning to the biggest stage in Tokyo after stepping away from tennis during the French Open, as a "huge inspiration".

"A couple of days ago I watched her whole docu-series on Netflix and it really shined a light on it. It's like, wow, she's one of the greatest athletes in the world and she took a step back and now look at her, she's back here at the Olympics, dominating. So sometimes it is OK to take a back seat – even at the most important meet." Now, Biles's name is added to the list of athletes inspiring others to put their own wellbeing above the demands of their sport and society. In October 2021, ahead of the winter Olympics in the New Year, figure skater Nathan Chen said that Biles's decision had given "all the athletes a sense of peace" and had opened a door they didn't think was there. "I think what Simone did at the last Olympics was extraordinarily inspirational and really just allowed all athletes to feel like, 'Hey, we are important as people, not just as athletes'," he said. "I didn't even realize that was an option, what she decided to do, and I was like, 'Wow, that actually makes me feel a lot better about who I am as an athlete, too.' Knowing that, when it comes down to it, I can choose my destiny." It is this legacy, her contribution to halting the abuse of Larry Nassar and pushing for change across USA Gymnastics, that will outshine the medals.

KHALIDA POPAL

"The Afghanistan women's national [football] team was built to fight against the Taliban and against the Taliban ideology, against the people that took the right to education and the right to social participation from women and kept women in silence, in dark houses, unable to leave, imprisoned," Khalida Popal told the *Guardian* in 2021. "The foundation of the team, of which I was one of the founders, was a way of activism for us, a way to stand up and send a message to the Taliban that the women of Afghanistan stand together."

The journey of the Afghanistan women's national team has been an arduous one and, at the heart of the desire to play, has been a desire to resist. In Afghanistan, women's football is life and death and, for Popal, fighting for the right for women to play has come at huge personal cost alongside the sporting and political gains.

Having become the first woman to work for the Afghanistan Football Federation, in the finance department, Popal had a profile and her advocacy for women's football saw her targeted. In 2011, fearing for her safety, she was forced to flee the country. This was the second time Popal had left everything behind; as a child, her family crossed the border into Pakistan following the rise of the Taliban returning after their removal from power. This time though, she was alone.

"I thought I have to leave otherwise I would be shot," she said. "I decided overnight. I didn't tell anyone I was going, just my father and my mother. It was a very tough time. I didn't know what to

pack. I didn't know when I would come back or where I would end up. I just took my bag with my computer and one picture of the team. I didn't take my football kit. I took nothing else.

"I didn't have time to get in touch with my teammates, they didn't know why I suddenly disappeared. I didn't tell them exactly what had happened to me for a very long time, I didn't want them to feel scared, I didn't want them to give up because they always saw me as a leader, a powerful person who stood up for them."

She travelled under the radar to India, staying on the move, before she reached an asylum centre in Norway and then moved to another in Denmark. While on the move, she still organized the team and once settled in Denmark, she continued to help progress women's football in Afghanistan from afar, setting up national team camps and recruiting sponsors. She also launched her own organization, Girl Power, that uses sport to help refugee girls find a release.

In 2018, when confronted by the sexual and physical abuse of players on the team, at a training camp in Jordan, Popal, along with the team's US coaches Kelly Lindsey and Haley Carter, sought help through FIFA and the Asian Football Confederation, but the response was slow from the former and non-existent from the latter.

By December, after many months of evidence gathering, Popal spearheaded the exposure of the abuses suffered by members of the women's national team at the hands of the president of the Afghanistan Football Federation in the *Guardian*. In June 2019, Keramuddin Karim was banned for life from football-related activities by FIFA and fined a million Swiss francs.

The team was thrown into turmoil once more when the US announced its withdrawal from Afghanistan in 2021, ceding control to the Taliban.

Suddenly the WhatsApp messages poured in from desperate former

"EVERYTHING IS REPEATING ITSELF. THESE YOUNG GIRLS, THEY ARE SO BEAUTIFUL AND YOUNG, IT'S JUST SO UNFAIR WHAT IS HAPPENING TO THEM."

Khalida Popal

teammates. Once more, Popal swung into action, working with the players' union FIFPRO and her connections. They helped pull together a team that embarked on a phenomenal rescue of hundreds of Afghan women athletes who were at risk because of their defiance through playing sport. It was a familiar process for Popal and her allies. They first got players through Taliban checkpoints with hidden documents, took them to the perimeter of Kabul airport, where they were plucked to safety from the crowds and sewers by military personnel with whom they had connected. Finally, they led the players to the Pakistan border and crossed it.

"I had to tell players they needed to choose which family member to take with them," said Popal. "It was awful. My voice was shaking. I said: 'Listen, my beautiful sisters, I understand. I understand how tough it is. I made this call many years ago. To survive. I left my family behind. I know how painful it is.'

"When I left my country my grandfather said: 'you're not coming back, right? We will not meet each other again,' and he started crying. He was my role model. My grandfather was a feminist, and he was the love of my life.

"When I looked into his eyes I was not able to say goodbye. I said: 'Listen, we will meet again,' knowing that I couldn't. I lost my grandfather and never managed to see him. Every time he would say to me on the phone: 'You promised that we will meet again.'

"Everything is repeating itself. These young girls, they are so beautiful and young, it's just so unfair what is happening to them. It's so unfair."

EMMA RADUCANU

When Emma Raducanu was given a wildcard place in the Wimbledon 2021 main draw, attention was drawn her way. Wins over Vitalia Diatchenko and top-50 opponents Markéta Vondroušová and Sorana Cîrstea helped her to become the youngest British woman to reach a Grand Slam last 16 in the Open Era at 18 years and 239 days old.

During her fourth-round match on Court One with Ajla Tomljanović, which she was losing 4–6, 0–3, she had difficulty breathing and was forced to retire from the match. She received a huge outpouring of support following her exit, but controversial journalist and broadcaster Piers Morgan criticized the praise and attacked her for not being able to "handle the pressure", told her to "toughen up" and dismissed suggestions that she was "brave". It was a revolting take on the Grand Slam debutante who had been sitting her A-Level exams two months prior and had not had a chance to prepare properly for staying the course in the competition.

"It's funny because at the beginning, when I was packing to come into the bubble, my parents were like, 'Aren't you packing too many sets of match kit?'", she said during the run.

"I think I'm going to have to do some laundry tonight, but I think they have a laundry service at the hotel so I'm all good, guys!"

The struggle at Wimbledon and the furore whipped up by Morgan and his ilk would have impacted the most senior professional. Yet, one month later, the teenager was in the US, losing in the first round of the Silicon Valley Classic before reaching the final of the WTA 125 event in Chicago. To play in US Open, Raducanu had go through the

qualification tournament, which is three rounds. She won her three matches in straight sets to make the main draw before going on a truly incredible run to the final without dropping a single set. As she progressed, she climbed the world rankings, became British No. 1 and captured the spotlight across the pond.

A staggering 9.2 million people in the UK watched the first all-teenage women's singles final at the US Open since 1999 live on Channel 4, while in the US more people tuned in for the women's final than they did for the men's. Her two-set victory over Canadian Leylah Fernandez meant she became the first qualifier to win a Grand Slam tournament and the first British woman to reach a US Open final since Virginia Wade in 1968.

She was an overnight superstar. Swapping Bromley for the Met Gala and courting brand after brand desperate for a piece of the new queen.

Almost immediately, however, she was subjected to sexist criticism. With her life upended, transformed forever, she struggled to replicate her US Open form as she sought a new coach and grappled with the interest from the media and fans.

"The big thing for young players is distractions," England rugby coach Eddie Jones said in relation to fly-half Marcus Smith, a young, rising star in England. "Distractions can be the exposure they get in the media, the praise and criticism they get, groups of agents who see this guy as the next big thing.

"THE HISTORY OF MALE SPORT IS OF HOW MANY ATHLETES HAVE PROSPERED AND DONE OTHER THINGS THAT THEY LIKE IN THEIR LIVES."

Kate Richardson-Walsh

"There's a reason why the girl who won the US Open [Raducanu] hasn't done so well afterwards. What have you seen her on? The front page of *Vogue*, the front page of *Harper's Bazaar*, whatever it is, wearing Christian Dior clothes.

"He [Smith] is grounded, but they all start off grounded. No one starts with their feet off the ground or they don't get in the team, or they don't win a US Open. But there's this flood of distractions that comes in that makes you ungrounded."

It was an unnecessary take and Women's Sport Trust ambassador Kate Richardson-Walsh – an Olympic Games hockey gold medallist – blasted the take as uninformed and sexist.

"Why is it negative for women to have money and connections with brands and businesses?" she asked. "The message is to focus on one thing, you can't multitask, you can't have it all.

"The history of male sport is of how many athletes have prospered and done other things that they like in their lives," she said.

The comments from Jones, though, meant the young star had to field questions about her commitment shortly after pulling off one of the most incredible wins in tennis history and have it consistently questioned.

"I made it very, very clear to every single person in my team that I was not going to cancel one training session or practice session for any off-court commitments," Raducanu said on the eve of the Upper Austria Ladies Linz tournament in November 2021.

"That was a non-negotiable for me. I wanted to make sure that that is my priority and it is. So, everyone's clear about that. But it's just managing my time with the commitments around that. Even if it's not off-court events or whatever, I'm still doing my WTA rookie hours, for example."

To be frank, whether Raducanu chooses to focus on her tennis or her off-court commitments, it is entirely up to her and whichever decision she makes does not need defending.

HILARY KNIGHT

"You have to continuously show up every single day, having that hunger of wanting to win and wanting to get better, both individually and collectively," Hilary Knight told *USA Today* shortly before she left for the Beijing 2022 Winter Olympics Games. "And I think that's the hardest thing in a team sport, right? You come from different backgrounds and you're working towards this common goal, but everyone needs to be aligned, especially when it matters."

Knight knows what it takes to win. The ice hockey superstar was preparing for her fourth Winter Olympics. She made her debut at the Games in 2010 in Vancouver, having taken a year out from the University of Wisconsin to join Team USA as the youngest member of the team at 20 years and 217 days old. That year she won a silver medal with the team, won another in 2014, finally had a gold medal hung round her neck at Pyeongchang in 2018 and won silver once more in 2022.

Women's ice hockey was introduced at the Nagano 1998 Winter Olympics, when Knight was eight, but she knew she would get there even before there was a competition. Her mother told her that when she was younger, she "turned to my grandmother and I was like, 'I'm playing hockey in the Olympics.' And at that time women's hockey wasn't in the Olympics. I was this crazy child that was like, 'I'm going to the Olympics'," she told *People* magazine in January 2022.

Ice hockey became Knight's sport when her family

relocated from California to Chicago. "I was sort of a late bloomer in the sport," she said. "I was just obsessed with the game and just wanted to get better. I couldn't even lift the puck until maybe two years or a year before high school.

"I wasn't great by any means, but I was just so hungry to get better that I think that helped me come into my own when I finally developed as a player."

Now, Knight is one of the most decorated players in the history of women's ice hockey. In addition to her four Olympic medals, she has won eight IIHF World Women's Championship titles (the first one when she was 17 in 2007), has three runners-up medals, and she holds the record for the most goals scored in the competition's history (47) and has 80 points for the US, an all-time record in the tournament.

At university she was the NCAA top scorer in her second year, with 45 goals and 83 points in 39 games. She is also Wisconsin's all-time leader in goals, 143, and points, 262. Knight became a professional hockey player with the Boston Blades, playing in the Canadian Women's Hockey League, and helped the team to a first title.

In 2014 she became the first female non-goaltender to practise with a men's National Hockey League side when she took to the ice with the Anaheim Ducks. In 2015 the National Women's Hockey League was formed in the US and Knight swapped to Boston Pride to compete in the tournament's inaugural season.

In 2018 she returned to the CWHL with Les Canadiennes de Montreal but the league folded after the 2018–19 season.

The forward has been vocal advocate for the professionalization of women's hockey and equality. "The NWHL was not ready to support us in the ways we needed and deserved," she told *Just Women's Sport*. "In the beginning I gave it time, and then I just

"YOU HAVE TO CONTINUOUSLY SHOW UP EVERY SINGLE DAY, HAVING THAT HUNGER OF WANTING TO WIN AND WANTING TO GET BETTER. "

Hilary Knight

realized that it was never going to grow into the league that could support its athletes.

"I knew the CWHL wasn't the answer either, but it provided a more competitive environment and potential stability. But months later, the CWHL ended up folding, which was a heartbreak in itself, but it allowed a handful of us to take a step back and ask ourselves: what are we doing here?"

Now, she is pushing for change and helped form the Professional Women's Hockey Players' Association, a five-team league with two teams in the United States and three in Canada.

"This is for the future of the game," she said. "We're trying to build something that's bigger and better than what is currently out there. Not only for ourselves but also for the younger girls who dream of playing professional hockey. We think change is necessary, and that is ultimately why we're not playing in any league in North America right now.

"It's a visibility issue, rather than a product issue. If we can continue to improve our visibility, fans will show up, they'll turn on their TVs, because the product is there. And I'm quite confident with that. If you look at where women's ice hockey is on growth charts and how it's developing in North America, even if you just look at the youth level, it's pretty outstanding. We're moving in the right direction. And we're all very excited about where the sport can go."

KAIYA
MCCULLOUGH

"This is probably the most terrified I've been about something in a long time," wrote former Washington Spirit player Kaiya McCullough on her social media channels. "It's taken me a year to process, but I'm grateful for the strength I've found during this year to get to where I'm at. I'm a firm believer that speaking out when things are wrong and unjust is the only way forward, and my hope is that this is the first step in serious change for players elsewhere.

" I don't play soccer anymore. I don't know if I ever will. But I hope that by sharing my story, nobody else will have to feel small. Thanks for the support."

That morning McCullough had gone on the record in the *Washington Post*, exposing a culture of verbal abuse and bullying and racism under Washington Spirit head coach Richie Burke.

"I was 100 percent in a situation where I was being emotionally abused by Richie," McCullough said in that interview. "He created this environment where I knew I wasn't playing as well because I was so, so scared to mess up and be yelled at. It crippled my performance, and it made me super anxious. He made me hate soccer."

McCullough had thrived while on an athletic scholarship at UCLA. In 2017, her sophomore year, she helped the team reach the College Cup championship, where they suffered a 3–2 defeat to Stanford.

She was also finding her voice politically and, that year, was one of the first college students to join NFL player Colin Kaepernick in kneeling during the national anthem during games to protest racial injustice and police brutality – she had already stopped saying the Pledge of Allegiance in high school because she did not feel the flag represented all Americans.

She did not miss a game in California, making 92 starts to become the joint fifth-most capped player in the history of women's football at the university. In 2019 she was named the PAC-12 scholar-athlete of the year and received the Athletic Director's Academic Excellence Award.

"My UCLA experience definitely shaped me and my unwavering confidence in myself," McCullough said in an interview with her university. "That's allowed me to move forward in my career on the field as well as off the field. It empowered me to speak my mind and speak my truth in all areas of my life."

The young defender was the 32nd overall pick in the 2020 NWSL draft, but her experience in her maiden professional season sapped her joy for the game so much she "dreaded having to go on the field" and, with nowhere to turn, she was eventually forced to step away from the game entirely, though she did spend a very short period playing in Germany's second tier with Würzburger Kickers.

McCullough was not the only player to shine a light on the inappropriate behaviours of coaches in the women's professional game in the US. In September 2021 two former Portland Thorns players, Mana Shim and Sinead Farrelly, supported by US women's international forward Alex Morgan, detailed the emotional abuse and sexual coercion they had suffered by then head coach of the team, Paul Riley, who, at the time of the publication of the allegations by the Athletic, was head coach of North Carolina Courage. Riley and Burke were both fired because of the allegations. In Seattle, OL Reign coach Farid Benstiti was asked to resign after

"THE BEST WAY TO PROTECT THE SANCTITY OF SOCCER IS TO TRUST THE PEOPLE WHO PLAY IT."

Kaiya McCullough

being accused of the verbal abuse of players, including Lindsey Horan, who accused him of body-shaming her. Meanwhile, Racing Louisville sacked Christy Holly for cause, with the local TV station WDRB reporting on complaints of a toxic culture, and Rory Dames was fired by Chicago Red Stars over reports of abuse.

Importantly, the brave stance of the players who came forward triggered a wave of solidarity among players and the support of fans, who rallied around them but also campaigned for really meaningful change.

In October 2021, the NWSL commissioner Lisa Baird was forced to resign because of the organization's mishandling of the accusations and Marla Messing was appointed as interim commissioner. Less than 10 days later, the NWSL players association announced that the NWSL had met all of the union's demands for reforms that would prevent incidents of abuse from happening and put in place reporting mechanisms.

"It's our duty to build a sport where trauma isn't the price for playing the game we love," said McCullough, in a column for the *Washington Post*. "It's our duty to demand conditions that allow players not merely to get by, but to thrive and rejoice. I alone don't have all the answers, but I know that the path charted by toxic coaches, owners and managers led us away from that ideal.

"Players, current and former, have been calling the shots for just a short while, but look at what progress has been made. The best way to protect the sanctity of soccer is to trust the people who play it."

SUN WEN

That Sun Wen won the FIFA Golden Ball and scored seven goals to earn the FIFA Golden Boot at the 1999 FIFA Women's World Cup in the United States, the competition that catapulted the winning US women's national team into the spotlight, speaks to just how remarkable a football player the China international was.

Sun's father, Sun Zonggao, played football for fun when she was young and he would take her to watch men's league matches in China. Little did he know he was feeding the ambitions of a child who picked up a ball at 10 and went on to become one of the greatest women to play the game.

Aged 16, the dynamic forward joined Shanghai SVA in the Chinese women's league in 1989. Her talents were quickly picked up by the national team and she made her debut a year later before going on to take part in four World Cups.

The first came in 1991, the inaugural tournament, which China exited at the quarter-final stage with a 1–0 defeat to Sweden. "My greatest memory from the World Cup is when I competed in my first tournament in Guangdong, China," she told FIFA.tv.

"I still remember the national anthem playing before our first match. I was so nervous I didn't know what to do. All I could think was … breathe. It was such an inspirational and exciting moment. For a young footballer, it was the biggest stage."

In 1995, China suffered a semi-final defeat to Germany but, four

years later, she did everything except grasp the trophy, as China suffered penalty shoot-out heartache. "It was a really great experience in my life, unforgettable for the players," she said in an interview on FIFA.tv "Even now I feel like I was dreaming. What was important is that we pushed women's football to a higher level."

The following year she was named FIFA's joint Female Player of the Century alongside US forward Michelle Akers. That year, Sun was the first draft pick for the inaugural season of the Women's United Soccer Association, what was the first ever women's professional league in the America. She stayed in the US with Atlanta Beat for two years. Her first season was interrupted by knee and ankle injuries, but she still had an impact. In the League's semi-final against the Philadelphia Charge, Sun scored a penalty and provided an assist for Cindy Parlow as the Beat came from behind to earn a 3–2 win. In her second season, she scored four times and helped the Beat reach the play-offs but they were knocked out at the semi-final stage. She was known for visiting the homes of Chinese fans for dinner. "Everyone wanted her over because to these people, Michael Jordan had come to their home," said Atlanta coach Tom Stone.

After that second season in Atlanta, she returned to Shanghai SVA in order to prepare for the 2003 World Cup.

Despite her huge impact on the game, Sun's name is not as widely known as it perhaps should be. Accolades though have never been the aim.

"I am not obsessed with titles and honours. To me, the valuable memories are the fantastic teamwork, the atmosphere in the stadium and the interactions with fans. My teammates and I, we still relish these precious memories."

However, the ever-humble Sun, who is now a vice president of the Chinese Football Federation, was a rare talent. Her former coach, Ma

"I WAS SO NERVOUS I DIDN'T KNOW WHAT TO DO. ALL I COULD THINK WAS... BREATHE. IT WAS SUCH AN INSPIRATIONAL AND EXCITING MOMENT. FOR A YOUNG FOOTBALLER, IT WAS THE BIGGEST STAGE."

Sun Wen

Liangxing once said: "She's the equivalent of Maradona, with the long shot and passing of Fígo, and the vision of Zidane."

Now, the goal is restoring the Chinese women's national team to their former position of one of the world's best teams.

"The administrative position requires a holistic view, an open mind and close coordination. From the bottom of my heart, I miss those days on the pitch as it was to me, a place of happiness," she said of her new role.

"We have seen the rise of European women's football not only through results, but also in tactical performance. Compared to my generation, a significant symbol of women's football in this era is that there are many brilliant players in every position, meaning Asian teams including China PR will face bigger challenges.

"Only high-level and high-quality matches can improve players. Organizing competitions, especially a professional league, is the key to boost the game. The FIFA Women's World Cup in France also showed the innovation of the women's football landscape. As football administrators in Asia, we need to promote our competitions with innovative ideas."

RACHAEL
HEYHOE FLINT

"Girls don't play cricket," said the policeman, looking down at a young Rachael Heyhoe. She had been playing with her friends and brother in the street outside their home and they had been forced to stop by the policeman, who admonished them for blocking the road. He took down their names, but not Heyhoe's. "I reached up, tapped him on the shoulder and pointed out that I had been playing cricket, too," she remembered in her autobiography. "His answer was most pitying ... which was about as devastating a blow to my pride as anyone could have delivered."

Cricket was not Heyhoe's only sport; as a child she played bicycle polo, football and cricket on the streets of Wolverhampton where she grew up and later took up hockey, rounders, and netball, as well as trying to join boys' cricket and football teams where she could.

Her parents were PE teachers and her father Geoffrey played hockey and cricket, with Rachael acting as the scorer beyond the cricket boundary. When she was 11, Geoffrey's cricket club, Wolverhampton Technical College, was a player down, so Heyhoe Flint was brought in.

"Amazingly, I soon found myself marked down to bat at No. 11, and had to go out to the crease to stave off defeat," she said. "The

"THE PADS REACHED MY WAIST AND THE BAT FELT LIKE A TREE TRUNK."

Rachael Heyhoe Flint

pads reached my waist and the bat felt like a tree trunk, but the men were kind enough to bowl me a few slowish half-volleys, and to everyone's surprise I managed to score two or three undefeated runs and save the game."

At secondary school, a trip to watch the Midland women's team play a New Zealand team at Edgbaston, led by PE teacher and cricket and hockey player Mary Greenhalgh, was a game-changer for the young Heyhoe.

"This was euphoria for me. Not only were we missing school lessons to watch cricket, but it was women's cricket, played at a very high standard," she said.

"As I studied the game at Edgbaston, I made up my mind that this was the life for me. I came away with an image of an exciting, challenging life, travelling the world playing cricket, meeting people. It seemed everything I wanted out of life and I think it was there and then that I determined I must play cricket for England women – though if the truth were known, I wasn't even sure whether England had a women's cricket team."

That child would become one of the most influential women in the history of cricket, both as a player and administrator.

As a batter, she averaged 45 in 22 Test matches, scoring 1,594 runs, and averaged 58 in One Day International matches. As captain of England for 12 years, from 1966 to 1978, she won 19 of 21 matches and was never on the losing team. Heyhoe also hit the first six in a women's Test match in 1963, at The Oval against Australia.

In 1971, the year she married Derrick Flint, her plans for a women's World Cup were formulated with her millionaire friend Jack Hayward. He coughed up £40,000 to help bring the best players from around the world to England to compete two years later. After the final match, against Australia at Edgbaston, Heyhoe Flint lifted the first World Cup

"I THINK IT WAS THERE AND THEN THAT I DETERMINED I MUST PLAY CRICKET FOR ENGLAND WOMEN'S CRICKET TEAM."

Rachael Heyhoe Flint

trophy. In the game she scored 64 runs.

In 1976, she batted for eight and a half hours across the third and fourth days of the final Test to save England from defeat. But maybe her proudest moment came on August 4

that year when Heyhoe Flint led the England team out at Lord's in the Women's One Day International series against Australia. She had long campaigned for England to play at "the home of cricket" and this was the first women's match played at the historic ground.

Away from sport, she swapped teaching PE for journalism and worked for the *Wolverhampton Express and Star* and, in 1967, started at the *Daily Telegraph*, where she worked as a freelancer for 23 years. She was the first female sports presenter on ITV's *World of Sport*.

Heyhoe Flint applied for membership of the previously "men-only" Marylebone Cricket Club, the former governing body of English and world cricket and whose home ground is Lord's. In 1999, she was one of the first 10 women admitted to the club as an honorary life member. She became an MCC committee member and then a trustee. Away from cricket, she was a director of Wolverhampton Wanderers FC and an ex-officio vice-president of the club.

Among the other honours bestowed on Heyhoe Flint were an MBE in 1972, OBE in 2008, she entered the House of Lords as a Conservative Party peer in 2010 and invested as a life peer in 2011. She was the first woman inducted into the International Cricket Council Hall of Fame and in 2021, four years after her death, the MCC announced it was naming a gate – replacing the North Gate – at Lord's after her.

CONCLUSION

When I was a child, growing up on a council estate in north London, my sporting idols were men – Thierry Henry, Dennis Bergkamp, Ian Wright, Lleyton Hewitt, Michael Schumacher, Tiger Woods and Colin Jackson (yes, I was born in the late 1980s). I would peel the backs off the Panini stickers and place the faces of male footballers into my Premier League albums.

I would walk down to the newsagent's on the edge of my estate, with a few coins rattling in my pocket, and pick up the Sunday newspapers for my dad, staring at the faces of the male athletes on the back pages as I weaved my way back through the blocks and up to our fourth-floor two-bed flat. I wore boys' football shirts and shorts, cutting out the netting from shorts, because kits for girls didn't exist. I would wear my hair up, in a tight ponytail, and wear a baseball cap, to try and fit into a world that found my presence and interest to be a novelty.

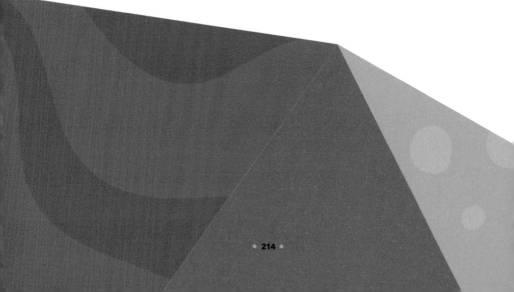

Yet, I was lucky, because I did see female athletes. Arsenal Ladies trained for a short period across the road from my estate in Shoreditch Park. The team were at the parades of the double-winning men's teams with their own trophies in tow. I worshiped Denise Lewis, Paula Radcliffe and Venus and Serena Williams. But, competing in seasonal events, they weren't in my everyday consciousness, and women's football was not covered week-to-week. Their time in the spotlight and dominating headlines was fleeting. Instead, the daily and weekly sporting news was filled with the Premier League, the England men's team, the Formula One season and other men's sports.

That is changing. Now, women's football can be found online and in newspapers daily. Women's domestic football in England is shown on Sky and the BBC. Women's rugby, tennis, athletics, golf and other women's sports are all benefiting from an increase in column inches as the media begins to recognize that the reciprocal role it played in the development of men's sport could be similarly beneficial both to itself and women's sport in the long term.

Meanwhile, the likes of Naomi Osaka, Serena Williams, Megan Rapinoe, Simone Biles and others are huge celebrities away from their sports as much as they are pioneering athletes in their individual fields.

These changes have not been automatic but are reflective of changes in attitude to women in society more generally. In recent years, we have seen numerous campaigns for women – demanding reproductive rights, challenging the gender pay gap, protesting deaths in police custody, fighting back against sexual abuse – and as society has shifted because of these movements, sport has been impacted and been a part of the change.

We are on the cusp of a really transformative time for sports, forcing people to reflect deeply on their values and purpose. The 91,553 fans who filed into the Camp Nou to watch Barcelona's European champion women's team play rivals Real Madrid in a UEFA Champions League quarter-final in March 2022 is both the beginning and a glimpse at the future potential of women's sport.

What is important now is that we savour, record and value the stories of this tranche of pioneering women in sport and make sure their journeys and histories are not lost, as were those of so many of the past pioneers. It is also important that, as a part of this growing and invested-in movement, money is invested and work is done to salvage as many stories of those who paved the way as is possible. Hopefully, this book will play a small role in introducing some of the heroines of women's sport to a wider audience. Hopefully, too, it is not the last to do this.

WE ARE ON THE CUSP OF A REALLY TRANSFORMATIVE TIME FOR SPORTS, FORCING PEOPLE TO REFLECT DEEPLY ON THEIR VALUES AND PURPOSE.

INDEX

AUTHOR BIOGRAPHY

Suzanne Wrack is a women's football writer for the *Guardian*. She previously worked on the *Guardian* sports desk as a layout sub editor. She has worked as a Senior Broadcast Journalist for *BBC Sport*, a digital designer for *The Sunday Times*, and page artist for *Trinity Mirror*. Suzanne is passionate about sport and enjoys exploring the politics of sport. She has an interest in fan-owned football clubs and issues around discrimination in sport.

Suzanne is an accredited football reporter, member of the SJA, member of the Football Writers' Association and a member of Women in Football.

She was highly commended in the *Media Initiative of the Year* category at the 2018 Women's Sport Trust "Be A Game Changer" awards, shortlisted for the Football Supporters Association writer of the year in 2018, 2019, 2020, 2021 and 2022, shortlisted for sports

journalist of the year at the British Press Awards in 2019 and 2022 and was shortlisted for football journalist of the year at Sports Journalist Association awards and was the winner of the "Writing – Best Colour" category at the AIPS awards, all in 2019. She is on the expert panel which helps determine the Women's Super League player of the month and is on the panel for the Women's Super League Hall of Fame.

Suzanne has a chapter included in *Football, She Wrote*, an anthology of women's football writers published in September 2021 and her first book, a social and political history of women's football, *A Woman's Game – The rise, fall and rise again of women's football* was published in June 2022 and on the William Hill Sports Book of the Year longlist. Suzanne co-wrote the non-fiction children's book *You Have the Power* with England captain Leah Williamson, which was published in March 2023.

ACKNOWLEDGEMENTS

I had just submitted the final draft of my debut book *A Woman's Game* and breathed a massive sigh of relief. Never, I swore, would I ever write a book again. A day later the phone rang and my agent Max Edwards, of Aevitas Creative, broached a new project. In my mind, I had already said no. It wasn't happening. Then the details of the project unravelled, it was this book, covering all sports, not just football, elevating the stories of women athletes that rarely have their stories told. On top of that, it would be illustrated. I have a passion for art and design, I studied Architecture at university, and the project was ticking boxes I didn't know I needed ticking.

So, thank you Max and thank you Millie Acers and Isabel Wilkinson of Welbeck Publishing, who approached Max to ask about me taking this book on.

It wasn't always easy, so little information about important women in the history of sports exists, but that's exactly why something like this is worth doing.

When I told my husband Michael about this new project, I was worried he would divorce me. Writing books while working full-time, and as parents, is not easy and we were all looking forward to a break. That break hasn't come yet, but Michael and our son James have weathered the writing storm and bent over backwards to help me make things happen.

Meanwhile, the rest of the family have stepped up and stepped in, to help with childcare and dog-sitting.

They say it takes a village to raise a child, it also takes a village to write a book.